Against Physicalism, Annihilationism, and Conditionalism

BOOKS BY JAMES D. QUIGGLE

DOCTRINAL SERIES

Biblical History

Adam and Eve, a Biography and Theology
Angelology, a True History of Angels

Essays

Biblical Essays
Biblical Essays II
Biblical Essays III
Biblical Essays IV

Marriage and Family

Marriage and Family: A Biblical Perspective
Biblical Homosexuality
A Biblical Response to Same-gender Marriage

Doctrinal and Practical Christianity

First Steps, Becoming a Follower of Jesus Christ
A Christian Catechism (with Christopher McCuin)
Why and How to do Bible Study
Thirty-Six Essentials of the Christian Faith
The Literal Hermeneutic, Explained and Illustrated
The Old Ten In the New Covenant
Christian Living and Doctrine
Spiritual Gifts
Why Christians Should Not Tithe

Dispensational Theology

A Primer On Dispensationalism
Understanding Dispensational Theology
Covenants and Dispensations in the Scripture

Dispensational Soteriology

Dispensational Eschatology, An Explanation and Defense of the Doctrine

Rapture: A Bible Study on the Rapture of the New Testament Church

Antichrist, His Genealogy, Kingdom, and Religion

God and Man

God's Choices, Doctrines of Foreordination, Election, Predestination

God Became Incarnate

Life, Death, Eternity

Did Jesus Go To Hell?

Against Physicalism, Annihilationism, and Conditionalism

Small Group Bible Studies

Elementary Bible Principles (with Linda M. Quiggle)

Counted Worthy (with Linda M. Quiggle)

COMMENTARY SERIES

The Old Testament

A Private Commentary on the Bible: Judges

A Private Commentary on the Book of Ruth

A Private Commentary on the Bible: Esther

A Private Commentary on the Bible: Song of Solomon

A Private Commentary on the Bible: Daniel

A Private Commentary on the Bible: Jonah

A Private Commentary on the Bible: Habakkuk

A Private Commentary on the Bible: Haggai

The New Testament

James Quiggle Translation New Testament (JQTNT)

The Gospels and Acts

A Private Commentary on the Bible: Matthew's Gospel
A Private Commentary on the Bible: Mark's Gospel
A Private Commentary on the Bible: Luke 1–12
A Private Commentary on the Bible: Luke 13–24
A Private Commentary on the Bible: John 1–12
A Private Commentary on the Bible: John 13–21
A Private Commentary on the Bible: Acts 1–14
A Private Commentary on the Bible: Acts 15–28

Other Works On the Gospels

Four Voices, One Testimony (a Gospel Harmony)
Jesus Said "I Am"
The Parables and Miracles of Jesus Christ
The Passion and Resurrection of Jesus the Christ
The Christmas Story, As Told By God
Christmas Card Theology and the Bible

Pauline Letters

A Private Commentary on the Bible: 1 Corinthians
A Private Commentary on the Bible: Galatians
A Private Commentary on the Bible: Ephesians
A Private Commentary on the Bible: Philippians
A Private Commentary on the Bible: Colossians
A Private Commentary on the Bible: Thessalonians
A Private Commentary on the Bible: Pastoral Letters
A Private Commentary on the Bible: Philemon

General Letters

A Private Commentary on the Book of Hebrews
A Private Commentary on the Bible: James
A Private Commentary on the Bible: 1 Peter
A Private Commentary on the Bible: 2 Peter
A Private Commentary on the Bible: John's Epistles
A Private Commentary on the Bible: Jude

Revelation

A Private Commentary on the Bible: Revelation 1–7
A Private Commentary on the Bible: Revelation 8–16
A Private Commentary on the Bible: Revelation 17–22

REFERENCE SERIES

James Quiggle Translation New Testament (JQT)
Dictionary of Doctrinal Words
Old and New Testament Chronology (With David Hollingsworth)
(Also in individual volumes: Old Testament Chronology; New Testament Chronology)

TRACTS

A Human Person: Is the Unborn Life a Person?
Biblical Marriage
How Can I Know I am A Christian?
Now That I am A Christian
Thirty-Six Essentials of the Christian Faith
What is a Pastor? / Why is My Pastor Eating the Sheep?
Principles and Precepts of the Literal Hermeneutic
(All tracts are in digital format and cost $0.99)

Formats

Print, Digital, Epub, PDF. Search "James D. Quiggle" or book title.

Against Physicalism, Annihilationism, and Conditionalism

Copyright Page

Against Physicalism, Annihilationism, and Conditionalism, copyright 2024, James D. Quiggle.

ISBN: 979-8-9871044-7-7

New Testament scripture quotations are from *James Quiggle Translation New Testament*, copyright 2023, James D. Quiggle.

Old Testament scripture quotations are the author's translation.

Table of Contents

Introduction 13
Christ Between Death and Resurrection 15
The Endless Conscious Suffering of the Unsaved 105
Conclusion 157
Sources 165

Introduction

In the past decade or so, Physicalism and Annihilationism received a revival by a pseudo-Christian group that wants to be known as "Evangelical Conditionalists." They self-identify as "Evangelical" because they believe they proclaim the gospel. They name themselves "Conditionalists" because their doctrine is immortality is conditional from birth to death, to be confirmed for some and denied to others after resurrection. Perhaps more simply, in the heresy that is Conditionalism, salvation is receiving immortality after resurrection.

Physicalism is the ancient doctrine that life is biological only, merely material, only physical, no immaterial or spiritual component at all. In Physicalism the person's existence ends at physical death. Annihilationism is the doctrine God punishes the unsaved with endless non-existence.

Evangelical Conditionalism has embraced Physicalism and Annihilationism to create a doctrine that all persons are born with conditional immortality; that all persons cease to exist at physical death; that all persons are brought back into existence by resurrection; that some resurrected receive immortality, which in the doctrines of Conditionalism is salvation; that some resurrected are not given immortality (not saved) and after a brief period of punishment are annihilated: made endlessly non-existent.

There are variations, as in all religious beliefs, but the description above incorporates the basic doctrines of Evangelical Conditionalism. There is no doctrine of sin, salvation is immortality after resurrection, and Jesus Christ was God who literally stopped being deity and became human.

The Evangelical Conditionalists have a web site, "Rethinking Hell." Like many pseudo-Christian groups much is said but little is of substance. Finding answers about their doctrines proved to be difficult. But some things were clear.

Conditionalists are not a unified group. Some believe human beings do not have a soul. Therefore, Jesus Christ did not have a soul.

Other Conditionalists believe human beings do have a soul but the soul ceases to exist after physical death, until brought back into existence at resurrection. The inevitable corollary is Jesus the Christ ceased to exist between his physical death and resurrection.

Other Conditionalists believe God the Son literally became a human being in the incarnation—God ceasing to be deity—but retained some of his deity powers.

Do not be deceived by this pseudo-Christian group. Scripture says they are not Evangelical, that salvation is during this mortal life, that the only condition for salvation is faith during this mortal life, and all human souls are naturally immortal at conception, having been created with the spirit essence "life" from the beginning, Genesis 2:7.

Let us begin.

Christ Between Death and Resurrection

Introduction

Was the person Jesus the Christ living, conscious, and active between his physical death and the resurrection of his physical body? The first purpose of this chapter is to demonstrate Jesus the Christ was living, conscious, and active during the time his physical body lay dead in the grave.

The doctrine of some Conditionalists is the non-existence of persons between physical death and resurrection. The doctrine of some Conditionalists is the human soul is unconscious and inactive (the doctrine of "soul sleep") between physical death and resurrection.

The second purpose of this chapter is (1) to demonstrate from Scripture that the Holy Spirit never teaches the non-existence of any angel or any human being at any time after their personal existence begins, and (2) demonstrate from Scripture all human souls are conscious and active between physical death and resurrection.

The doctrine of all Conditionalists is all unsaved souls, after final judgment (Revelation 20:11–15), will suffer for an undetermined period of time in the lake of fire and after will be annihilated by the lake of fire into a permanent state of non-existence. Chapter 2 will demonstrate from Scripture all human beings cast in the lake of fire continue endlessly in the lake of fire.

Defense and Proof

To demonstrate the doctrines of Evangelical Conditionalism do not agree with the teaching of Scripture as a whole, will require an in depth exploration of many diverse Christian and Evangelical Conditionalists' doctrines concerning the nature of human beings, sin, salvation, the incarnation, the everlasting nature of the Lake of Fire, and other related doctrines. I ask for the reader's patience and focus.

The Conditionalists' heresy, despite its claim to be Evangelical, is opposed to orthodox Christianity, as historically defined by the Scripture and the New Testament church. The Evangelical Conditionalists deny essential doctrines of the faith.

What is an essential doctrine of the faith? [Quiggle, *Thirty-six*, 3].

> An essential doctrine of the Christian faith is a fundamental truth drawn solely from the sixty-six canonical books of Scripture, the denial or absence of which does not conform to the biblical and apostolic Christian faith as it is expressed and defined by the Scripture.
>
> A simpler definition for popular use: A doctrine of Scripture which, when missing or denied, Christianity ceases to be the Christianity defined and exampled in the Scripture.
>
> The essential beliefs of the Christian faith are those which are the *sine qua non* (literally, "without which nothing"), that if missing or denied Christianity ceases to be genuine biblical apostolic Christianity.

To hold some essential doctrines, as the Conditionalists claim to do, but not hold all essential doctrines, is to fail the test of orthodox Christianity.

The doctrines of the "Evangelical Conditionalist-Physicalist-Dualists-Annihilationists" (see below) includes the beliefs that life is material only, that God stopped being God in the incarnation, that the Christ ceased to exist between his death and resurrection, that the consequence of rejecting God and God's salvation is annihilation, and other critical essential doctrines of the faith having to do with sin, the Savior, and salvation, define Evangelical Conditionalism as heretical and cultic.

> Heresy. A deliberate denial of truth as revealed in the Scripture, development of an alternative belief, and teaching that alternative belief as though it was Scripture.
>
> Heretic. A person using heresy to establish a sect or religion in competition with Christianity, within or without the professing church.
>
> Cult. A religious organization calling itself Christian, whose doctrines differ significantly from historic orthodox biblical Christianity, as Christianity has been defined by the apostolic testimony in the New Testament Scripture, and in church councils, ca. AD 100–500, in those canons that conform to the apostolic testimony contained in the New Testament Scripture.

Necessary definitions. In this chapter, the word "eternal" is used of God as an increate being, thus without beginning or ending: eternal. The word "eternal" is also used of the kind of life God imparts to the saved, which is a quality of life in which God shares the communicable aspects of his life with the saved, in a degree suitable to finite beings.

The word "immortal" refers to the endless duration of human life: the human soul is naturally immortal once conceived; the human body will be resurrected immortal.

The word "endless" refers to a condition that once begun never ends. The human soul, once brought into existence by the processes of conception, is endlessly immortal. The human body, saved or unsaved, after resurrection (or rapture, 1 Corinthians 15:51–52; 1 Thessalonians 4:17), is endlessly immortal.

The punishment of the unsaved in the lake of fire is not eternal, because it has a beginning, but it is endless because it has no end. Annihilationism is not a Christian doctrine.

> Westminster Confession of Faith (WCF), Chapter 33, Of the Last Judgment, paragraph 2, "but the wicked, who know not God, and obey not the gospel of Jesus Christ, shall be cast into eternal torments, and be punished with everlasting destruction from the presence of the Lord, and from the glory of his power; Mat 25:41, 46; 2 Thes 1:9."

To the Conditionalists, the phrase "everlasting destruction from the presence of the Lord" means the punishment of the unsaved is endless non-existence. However, we are not left to the devices of others to know what those Christians who created the Confession meant by "everlasting destruction." David Dickson (1583–1663) wrote a commentary on the AD 1643 Confession.

His comments on chapter 33 of the WCF are in part as follows.

> Well then, do not the Socinians err, who define eternal death to be the extinguishing of the body and soul, maintain ... their whole punishment will be ...annihilation, that is, both body and soul turned into nothing? Yes. [Dickson, 239]

As a contemporary theologian he understand the historic orthodox theology of Christianity, and reflects that in the subtitle of his work, "The True Principles of the Christian Religion." But I digress. The whole matter will be discussed in chapter 2.

Diligent attention to these definitions will clarify the differences between what the Scripture teaches and what the Physicalist, Annihilationist, and Evangelical Conditionalist believe.

Defining Evangelical Conditionalism

What do Conditionalists believe? Some are pure Physicalists: life and mind are biological processes; there is no immaterial soul. Some are Dualists: life is both physical and spiritual: there is a soul. All want to be known as Evangelical Conditionalists: immortality of body and soul is conditional, to be confirmed for some and denied to others after resurrection. A doctrinal statement by one of the proponents of Evangelical Conditionalism gives some help.

> Evangelical Conditionalists also differ in terms of what we believe the Bible says about the constitution of human beings, and also about whether people are conscious in the intermediate state between death and resurrection. Some are anthropological physicalists or

materialists who believe human beings are physical creatures, the functioning of whose minds is dependent upon their living bodies. Others are substance dualists who believe human beings have immaterial souls, but that they lack consciousness between death and resurrection. Still others embrace a traditional body/soul dualism and contend that the immaterial souls of human beings live on consciously after death, until a resurrection of the body. [https://rethinkinghell.com/statement/ paragraph 8.4.]

Evangelical Conditionalism embraces all those views.

To call them Evangelical Conditionalist-Physicalist-Dualists-Annihilationists is a bit unwieldly, and as tedious to write as it is to read. I will identify them generally as Conditionalists, and particularly as different branches of the group come under consideration.

All Conditionalists, whether Physicalist, Substance Dualist, or Traditional Dualists incorporate four Scripture doctrines, with greater or lesser accuracy or denial, into their particular view.

The Conditionalist doctrines.

No human being is conceived with immortality in body and soul.

All human beings must experience resurrection after physical death.

Some human beings will be given immortal life in body and soul after resurrection.

Some human beings will be sent to the lake of fire after

resurrection to be punished and then annihilated.

Throughout this book I will provide links to Conditionalist doctrine (such as the "Statement" above) revealing their doctrine from an official source.

The Scripture doctrines.

> All human beings are conceived with immortal souls. Genesis 2:7; 5:3; Matthew 17:2; Luke 16:22–23; 2 Corinthians 5:8.
>
> All human beings must experience resurrection after physical death. Daniel 12:2; 1 Corinthians 15:12, 23; Revelation 20:4–6, 12–13.
>
> All human beings will be given immortal physical life after resurrection. Daniel 12:2; 1 Corinthians 15:12, 23; Revelation 20:4–6, 12–13.
>
> Some human beings will live endlessly in God's immediate and effective presence. Philippians 1:23; 1 Thessalonians 4:16–17; Revelation 19:7–9.
>
> Some human beings will be sent to the lake of fire to suffer endless punishment. Isaiah 66:24; Mark 9:43, 44, 46, 48; Revelation 20:11–15.

I will disprove the Conditionalist beliefs (exception: all must experience resurrection) with scripture and with reasoning based on sound principles of logic. Let us begin with a more detailed review of Conditionalist doctrine.

Defining Conditionalist Doctrine

I realize there is some repetition in these lists of beliefs, but because Evangelical Conditionalism embraces Physicalism, Dualism, and Annihilationism, it is necessary to define each point of view, lest some Conditionalist accuse me of misrepresentation.

All Conditionalists, whether Physicalist or Dualist, hold these beliefs in common.

>Immortality is not innate to human beings or angels.

>Immortality is conditioned upon belonging to Christ.

>Immortality is bestowed by God on those belonging to Christ after their resurrection.

>Immortality is not bestowed at any time on those not belonging to Christ.

>There is no salvation during physical life. The "gift" of immortality of body and soul after resurrection is salvation.

(A little below I will discuss what "belonging to Christ" means in Conditionalist doctrine, and how it affects the orthodox doctrine of salvation.)

>Those human beings who are not given immortality after resurrection will suffer an indeterminate duration of punishment in the lake of fire and then cease to exist.

>Endless punishment does not refer to the punishment itself, but to the outcome of the punishment, which is an endless non-existence.

Continuing with Conditionalist doctrine.

>Physicalist Conditionalists believe all human beings cease to exist at physical death and all are subsequently

recreated by resurrection. Those of the resurrected who are given immortality of body and soul—and thereby salvation—continue endlessly. Those not given immortality endure an indeterminate duration of punishment in the lake of fire and then are made endlessly non-existent.

Substance Dualist Conditionalists and Traditional Dualist Conditionalists believe all human beings continue to exist after physical death (either asleep [the Substance Dualist] or conscious and active [the Traditional Dualist]) and all are resurrected. Then, those resurrected who are given immortality of body and soul—and thereby salvation—continue endlessly. Those not given immortality endure an indeterminate duration of punishment in the lake of fire and then are made endlessly non-existent.

All Conditionalists subscribe to Conditionalism, aka "conditional immortality." Conditionalists believe immortality is, "a gift bestowed by God upon his children" after physical death and resurrection [https://rethinkinghell.com/explore/].

As noted above, receipt of immortality is salvation in Conditionalism; or using their own words, receipt of immortality "determines who is a child of God" [https://rethinkinghell.com/explore/].

Conditional immortality means no one, whether with a soul (Substance/Traditional Dualist) or without a soul (Physicalist), has innate immortality of either body or soul, until and if immortality of body and soul [salvation] is given to some as a gift by God after their personal death and resurrection.

The reader will have noticed the words "after physical death and resurrection" (two paragraphs above) are not part of the quote from the "Rethinking Hell" website. The reason is the site is a maze of articles that never quite touches on the subject of when immortality is granted. But that it is their doctrine is clear from the following statements

> God alone possesses immortality innately and therefore any other being who is immortal (imperishable, deathless) is so extrinsically, that is, as the result of a positive act of God.
> [https://rethinkinghell.com/explore/]

> Conditionalism is the view that life is the Creator's provisional gift to all, which will ultimately be granted forever to the saved and revoked forever from the unsaved. When the gift of life is ultimately granted forever, we call that immortality. We also call it eternal life. Salvation, on our view, is salvation to everlasting life with God. Simultaneously, it is salvation from a permanent death (termination of life forever; final loss of being).
> [https://rethinkinghell.com/2019/07/20/conditional-immortality-meaning-best-label/]

> In denying that all seek and receive the gift of eternal life, which we associate with immortality, we are denying universal immortality. We are denying that all

people ever to have lived will live forever. [https://rethinkinghell.com/2019/07/20/conditional-immortality-meaning-best-label/]

Conditionalism is the view that life is the Creator's provisional gift to all, which will ultimately be granted forever to the saved and revoked forever from the unsaved. [https://rethinkinghell.com/2019/07/20/conditional-immortality-meaning-best-label/]

(When, above, the Conditionalist says "God alone possesses immortality innately" that is confusing the increate eternality of God (Exodus 3:14; John 5:26) with a condition, immortality, only applicable to created beings.)

I will show Scripture teaches all human beings are naturally immortal in soul and will be made physically immortal after resurrection. As to salvation, the Scripture presents that all who have believed in the risen Jesus Christ as Savior during this mortal life are given the quality of eternal life as a present and endless possession, John 10:28, during this mortal life, and the regeneration of their human nature (born-again) as the result of a present and endless salvation, 1 Peter 1:22–23.

In Conditionalism there is no salvation until after the body is resurrected. How does a person qualify to receive immortal life in body and soul, and thereby salvation, in Conditionalism? "To receive this crown [of body-soul immortality], a person must belong to Christ." [https://rethinkinghell.com/2019/07/20/conditional-immortality-meaning-best-label/].

I cannot say how all Conditionalists understand how a person "belongs to Christ," but belonging to Christ is defined by one Conditionalist as, "All the sinners whom God had chosen 'before the foundation of the world to be holy and blameless before him in love,' [have] been chosen 'in Christ' (Eph 1:4)." [https://rethinkinghell.com/2016/07/17/what-did-jesus-suffer-for-us-and-for-our-salvation/]

I know I have labored this point because it is of critical importance. In Conditionalism, God chose a person to have faith in Christ (in this life? after resurrection?) and then be saved *after* his or her resurrection. Not discussed in the any articles I read is when the elect have their faith in Christ. Is it during physical life, or after resurrection?

What the Conditionalist does say, clearly and with certainty, is salvation in Conditionalism is receiving body-soul immortality *after* physical death and resurrection, and without that immortality existence does not continue. Therefore, in Conditionalism, salvation is receiving immortality, and therefore, in Conditionalism, salvation occurs after physical death, after bodily resurrection. Until then, no person can know if he or she is saved, contra 1 John 5:10–13.

Do not be deceived by the sound of words from the Conditionalist: those persons receiving body-soul immortality are not saved in the biblical sense. The Conditionalist's conditional immortality doctrine means the work of Christ on the cross was proleptic (anticipatory) of all salvations—all those believers in both Old and New Testaments, such as Moses, the prophets, the apostles, and every other person presented in Scripture as a believer in God as Savior—have not yet been saved because Christ's propitiation of God for human sin is, in the Conditionalist's doctrine, *not individually effective until after the individual is resurrected*. In Conditionalism, no one from the times of Adam and Eve to this present time, and continuing in to the yet-future, has been saved, because no one has been resurrected.

That this is the doctrinal position of the Conditionalist on salvation was affirmed in a debate, March 20, 2021, with Chris Date and Dr. Glenn Peoples defending the Conditionalist doctrine, opposing Dr. Keith Sherlin and Pastor Brannon Poore defending the biblical doctrine. See about the 1 hour, 43 minute mark at [https://www.youtube.com/watch?v=2UEXqxpp5FY].

I cannot say how all Conditionalists understand when saving faith occurs, but these two well-known Conditionalists, spokespersons for Evangelical Conditionalism, indicate saving faith occurs *after* physical death and resurrection, because "Christ's propitiation of God for human sin is not effective until the person is resurrected" (see debate video). That means because God's justice has not yet been satisfied for a person's sin until *after* the person has died and been resurrected, there is no basis in God's justice for God to give that sinner God's gift of grace-faith-salvation, Ephesians 2:8, until *after* that person's physical death and resurrection. Without God's gift there is no spiritual perception, 1 Corinthians 2:14, with which to understand the issues of sin, the Savior, and salvation. If salvation occurs after resurrection, then saving faith must occur after resurrection.

This is important. The orthodox Christian doctrine is God is able to act to save individuals from the first person Adam forward to the last person saved before the new heaven and earth, just because Christ's propitiation (aka: atonement) of God for human sin on the cross fully satisfied God's justice against sin.

The scriptures know no difference between the Old Testament and New Testament sinner when they say, "all human beings have sinned," and "Christ is propitiation for our sins." In the Scripture, an actual and effective, born-again, during this mortal life salvation, began with Abel. (Adam and Eve were born sinless, were never lost, so never saved; God acted remedially to restore them to fellowship after their sin: repentance, confession, restoration, 1 John 1:9. See Quiggle, *Adam and Eve*.)

The orthodox Christian doctrine is Christ's propitiation was and is effective from the moment God decreed Christ's merit as the only means to effect salvation, Ephesians 1:4, in the eternity past before the universe was created. The basis of salvation in any age of humankind is the propitiation of God made by Christ [Ryrie, *Dispensationalism*, 115]. God did not punish "the sins that are past" (Romans 3:25), i.e., the Old Testament peoples that believed (cf. Hebrews 2:17). Why? Because Christ's sufferings on the cross propitiated God for sins, Romans 3:24–25. Because God "loved us, and sent his son, a propitiation for our sins," 1 John 4:10.

Redefining what salvation is and when salvation occurs is only one of the essential doctrines of orthodox Christianity that marks any form of Conditionalism as false doctrine. Conditionalism is heretical, a sect teaching false doctrine within the New Testament church (versus apostate, leaving the New Testament church to teach a false view of Christianity), because they claim to remain within the orthodox New Testament church by identifying themselves as "Evangelical" Conditionalists [https://rethinkinghell.com/statement/]. But make no mistake, Conditionalism is not the orthodox Christian faith as defined in the Bible and by the New Testament church for almost 2,000 years.

Some Conditionalists fail to distinguish between hades (*hádēs*), a temporary place for unsaved human souls until final judgment, and the true hell, which is the lake of fire (*géenna*, aka Gehenna). In this chapter, the term "hell" means the lake of fire

(A word study of Jesus' use of the Greek words *hádēs* and *géenna* reveal *hádēs* is not the same as *géenna*, which is the true hell. See either of my books *Life, Death, Eternity*, or *Dispensational Eschatology*, for that word study).

Hades is a temporary location in the spirit domain for unsaved souls after physical death. Think of hades as the county jail where the convicted and sentenced await their final disposition in the endless prison, which is the lake of fire.

The Anthropological Physicalists or Materialists

The "Anthropological Physicalists or Materialists" doctrine (hereinafter Physicalist or Physicalism) is this: a human being ceases to have any kind of personal existence after physical death.

Let us clearly understand the word "person" is an oxymoron in Physicalism. In Physicalism, a "person" is nothing more than mental activity produced as an effect or byproduct of biological processes. There is no genuine person in the biblical sense, only neurons generating electrical impulses and chemical processes transmitting those impulses from one neuron to another. The effect of that biological activity is the pseudo appearance of a "person." When the biological activity stops, the "person" ceases to exist.

The Physicalist's concept of "person" is like saying the cookie jar itself produces the cookies inside the jar, and when the jar breaks, all the cookies the jar produced disappear, as though they never existed.

There is no immaterial soul in Physicalism. Physicalism teaches resurrection of the body to physical life, and thereby mental activity resumes: the "person" is re-formed by the renewed biological processes. Physicalism is a thoroughly materialistic doctrine. In Physicalism, the only difference between a human being and a rock is the human being is temporarily alive.

I have some questions for the Physicalist. When biological processes change due to illness, is a new "person" formed by the body; and is yet another person formed when the body is healed? Does mental illness form a new person? Is the former person restored should the mental illness be cured? Another question relates to physiology. All human physiology—that of each and every human being—biologically functions in the same manner. How, then, can there be individual effects—individually unique persons—from biologically similar processes? I don't find answers to these questions in Physicalism.

But we will accept Physicalism's irrationality of individually unique persons from the same biological processes, solely for the sake of discussing how their doctrines may or may not be relevant to the question that is the topic of this chapter, Christ living, conscious, and active between death and resurrection. Because Christ is the firstfruits, 1 Corinthians 15:20, i.e., he was the first human being to die and be resurrected to new life, his state between death and resurrection tells us the state of all humankind between death and resurrection: living, conscious, and active.

To discuss Physicalism in biblical terms, we must expose their dishonest use of the word "person." In the doctrine of Physicalism, the person is not genuine, it is a mental effect of the body's biology. Only the body is genuine, the person is a side effect, a byproduct of biology, ephemeral, here today, gone tomorrow. The spiritual consequences of Physicalism are the person is not a sinner, the body sins; the person is not saved, the body is saved; a person is not unsaved, the body is unsaved; the saved person is not given immortality, the saved body is given immortality; the unsaved person is not annihilated, the unsaved body is annihilated. The person is produced by the biological processes of the body, so whatever happens to the body affects the so-called person. These are the rational consequences of Physicalism's doctrine.

In Conditionalism, no person has immortality in body or soul during this mortal life. In Physicalist-Conditionalist doctrine, when the body, and therefore the "person," dies, he or she ceases to exist as a person, because the body that creates the person has died. Do not be fooled by the Physicalist-Conditionalist's disingenuous "it isn't non-existence, the body is continues to exist in the grave." Yes, the body continues to exist, but because in the Physicalist-Conditionalist's doctrine the "person" is produced as an effect of biological activity by the living body, when death has occurred that biological activity ceases to exist, and therefore the person created by the living body ceases to exist.

Some bodies when resurrected are given immortal physical life, which in any kind of Conditionalism is considered salvation. Other bodies are resurrected to mortal life, temporary punishment, and cessation of existence by annihilation of the body.

Here is a question: why inflict the denial of immortality twice upon the unsaved body, by resurrecting that unsaved body to a second judgment and a second death? And just what is that second death? The first death, the body's physical death, caused the non-existence of the "person." Is something more needed? Is that second death a complete annihilation of the body by reduction to subatomic particles? Or is that second death the unsaved body burned up in hell with ashes floating around in the universe? Regardless, in Physicalism the ephemeral "person" ceases to exist when the body ceases to exist, first at the physical death of the body, and then at a second death, which is the annihilation of the body in the lake of fire. But why the illogic of two deaths when the first death is annihilation, in Physicalist-Conditionalism?

The reason the Physicalist-Conditionalist has a resurrection of the body leading to a second death in the lake of fire is an attempt to appear scriptural. They cannot ignore the "second death" in Revelation 20:6, 14; 21:8, of the unsaved. Therefore, they must incorporate resurrection of the unsaved into their doctrine—but their doctrine has no rational reason for a resurrection of the unsaved to a second death. If God's justice is satisfied by the unsaved body *not* being confirmed in its conditional immortality through physical death, then why have a second death and second annihilation to reconfirm that denial?

In Physicalism, annihilation of the "person" occurs at physical death. There is no rationality to the Physicalist's process of annihilation-resurrection-annihilation. There is no rational reason for those punished by annihilation of the "person" through physical death to suffer a second annihilation, other than an inane effort to make their doctrine appear biblical. Physicalism seeks to preserve a façade of orthodoxy without the substance.

In Physicalism, the future for the saved body is confirmed immortality in heaven after resurrection. Why then should the saved body first experience annihilation of the "person" via physical death, which denies confirmation of their conditional immortality, and then be re-created to a confirmed immortal physical life and hence an immortal body producing a "person?"

There is no rationality to the Physicalist's process of annihilation-resurrection-immortality for the saved. Why not directly transition the believer from mortal life to confirmed immortal life at the time of physical death? The answer is, Physicalist-Conditionalism must in some manner incorporate the Scripture doctrine of resurrection, but they must also, in agreement with their doctrine, annihilate the biological mental effect (the "person") so the mortal body "belonging to Christ" may be resurrected to physical immortality.

If, as proposed by Physicalist-Conditionalism, the mind is

simply the byproduct of physical life, is the mind produced by an immortal saved body the same as the mind that had been produced by a mortal unsaved body? Remember, in Conditionalism all human beings are unsaved at physical death, with only the elect to be saved at resurrection. Looking to Physicalism's doctrines, the physiology of an immortal saved body must be of a different order than an unsaved mortal body. Is the now immortal body of a different mind, and therefore not the same person?

Physicalism will argue orthodox Christianity also teaches the saved continue endlessly in the physical body. That belief is typical of the way Physicalism in particular (and Conditionalism in general) misstates or distorts Scripture. Scriptural, orthodox, Christianity teaches every human being is a person: an independently existing immaterial soul possessing unconditional immortality from the moment of existence (I gave some scriptures above; I will show this from Scripture in another section, below). Scriptural Christianity teaches the material body, saved and unsaved, is not conceived conditionally immortal, but is fully mortal until resurrected, at which time the body of both saved and unsaved persons is made immortal.

In scriptural Christianity, the human soul is naturally immortal, living, conscious, and active after physical death. Only the body is re-created, that is, resurrected, from decomposed remains. Then the immortal soul is reunited with its resurrected and now immortal body, to live endlessly in union as immortal soul in the now immortal body. In scriptural Christianity, the believer's resurrected body is transformed to be immortal and incorruptible. In scriptural Christianity, the body of the unsaved person is resurrected to be immortal and corruptible, as suitable for endless punishment.

Physicalism also has problems with the Holy Spirit's work of regeneration (born-again) that is concurrent with salvation. In scriptural Christianity the immortal soul, which is the person, is born-again from sinner to saved during the person's physically mortal life. That is a spiritual event affecting the immaterial soul, not a physical process affecting the body's biology. Does the condition "born-again" exist in Physicalist-Conditionalism? If so, what, exactly, has been born-again if there is no immaterial soul; if a "person" is only an effect of biology? Does the Holy Spirit add a new biological process to the body to make the "person" born-again?

But, of course, in Physicalist-Conditionalism, there is no salvation until *after* resurrection, when immortality is bestowed; is there still regeneration? John 3:3, "Jesus responded and said to him, 'I tell you the truth, if anyone be not born from above, he is not able to see the kingdom of God.'" A question no variety of Conditionalism answers.

There is no salvation without the regeneration of the immaterial human nature in the immaterial soul. In scriptural Christianity, human nature is an immaterial essence, the attributes of human nature are the qualities of that essence. The same attributes of human nature are present in the unsaved as in the saved.

In the unsaved, the attribute sin directs all other attributes of human nature to serve self, not God. In the salvation-regeneration event of biblical Christianity (born-again), the attributes are repurposed to serve God, not self. The attribute holiness is added, and the attribute sin (added by Adam's sin) is relegated to a minor role (unceasing temptation). But—*an important but*—in Physicalism there is no immaterial human nature, only a biological byproduct that Physicalism pretends is a genuine "person." The question repeats: salvation in Physicalist-Conditionalism is something that affects the body, so just how is that body saved? How is that body born-again?

If being born-again means conditional immortality has been confirmed—but no, in Physicalist-Conditionalism confirmation of immortality occurs *after* resurrection. Conditionalism in general teaches, "To receive this crown [of confirmed immortality], a person must belong to Christ" (i.e., be one of God's elect) [https://rethinkinghell.com/explore/]. Is it the same for the Physicalist-Conditionalist?

Or is Physicalism salvation by works: what the body does or does not do. How can an effect of biological processes, the so-called "person," have faith? How can an effect of biology sin? What must a physical body do to deserve immortality? These are orphaned questions lacking answers from the Physicalist-Conditionalist. Physicalism cannot have it both ways. Either there is an independent entity, a person, joined in union with the physical body; or there is a biological effect of the physical body that only seems like a person, but in fact is not an independent entity.

The attempt by Physicalism to create mind from matter is merely verbal alchemy trying to reduce the intangibilities of sensation, emotion, thought, will, volition, sin, faith, etc., to tangibility (cf. Hodge, 2:43). Physicalism is an unproven theoretical doctrine without genuine life; zombie-like it stumbles about seeking whom it may devour.

Physicalism raises serious questions about the nature of God. Indeed, if all life is physical, then the living God must be physical, the universe his body, and all things not alive and all living beings are merely parts of that physical body of God; but that is a form of Pantheism, which the Physicalist-Conditionalist would strongly deny. But we will set this aside to pursue matters related to the physical living beings Physicalism says God created.

Is God, as Creator of the body, the culpable author of sin? Or does the body somehow act in some manner contrary to the biological processes designed by its Creator, in order to originate sin? For it is certain the so-called mind in Physicalism cannot sin independent of the body, because the mind in Physicalism is only an effect of the body's biology. Sin and salvation must be biological acts in Physicalism. If the biological processes become faulty—a physical or mental illness—is that sin? if the biological processes are proper, is there no sin?

How does a biological process amend, change, or delete some aspect of its biological processes and remain viable? In Physicalism, a thought or desire is simply an effect of some biological process, so the thought or desire to sin must originate in some biological process. (In scriptural Christianity thought originates in the immaterial soul and enters the material world through the soul's interaction with the body.) How can a biological process change itself? Answer: it cannot, biological processes are changed by influences external to the body's biology. Is God, then, the external influence that changes the biological process to create a sinner? May it never be! The question repeats: what is salvation for the body in Physicalism? Physicalist-Conditionalism apparently has no answer.

What is sin in Physicalism? Conditionalism acknowledges the fact of sin, but doesn't seem to have a doctrine of sin; at least not a doctrine that explains what sin means to the Anthropological Physicalist-Materialist. How did sin come into existence in Physicalism? These are the kind of questions abandoned on the doorstep of Conditionalism. Unfortunately, we must also leave them there, for they are not within the scope of this chapter, and neither Physicalism nor Evangelical Conditionalism provides answers.

I have briefly discussed Physicalist-Conditionalism to explore whether or not the Physicalist's doctrine is relevant to answer our question, "Was Jesus the Christ living, conscious, and active between his physical death and the resurrection of his physical body?" No, Physicalism is not relevant to the question. Physicalism cannot answer its own problems, let alone create an issue with Jesus Christ. Physicalism is yet another false doctrine waiting to be cast into the dustbin of history, and it is nothing more. Yet, there it is, snapping uselessly at the feet of Scripture, kept in check by the chains of its own improbabilities. The doctrines of Physicalism are wholly destructive to many essential Scripture doctrines, so we must continue to address it from time to time.

The Physicalist-Conditionalist also cannot ignore the scriptures (e.g., Colossians 2:9) that teach God the Son incarnated into a human body. But the different varieties of Conditionalism deal with the problem in different ways, which I will address in the next section. What is plain is in every variation of Physicalism, and therefore Physicalist-Conditionalism, the incarnation of God the Son in the human being Jesus of Nazareth ceases to exist when Jesus, the human component of the God-man, physically dies. That is because in Physicalism the person Jesus is not a genuine person, but merely and only a side effect, a byproduct, of biology! As we shall see, in Physicalist-Conditionalist doctrine, God the Son ceased to exist when Jesus died.

In relation to the "anthropological physicalists or materialists" of Conditionalism, the argument in this chapter is to show from Scripture that life is not the consequence of biological processes, that human beings are a union of the material and immaterial, and the incarnation of God the Son with the genuine human person Jesus of Nazareth continued without cessation between the death of the human body of the God-man and its resurrection.

The Substance Dualists and Traditional Dualists

In relation to the Conditionalist "substance dualists," my task is to show from Scripture the living immaterial immortal soul continues to be conscious and active during physical death. That includes the human component of the God-man. In relation to the "traditional body/soul dualism" there is no need for a counter argument, as concerns the topic of this chapter.

Answering the doctrines of Evangelical Conditionalism

Outline of the Rest of the Chapter

The diversity of beliefs within the Conditionalist camp affects the topic of this chapter, "Was Jesus the Christ conscious and active between his physical death and the resurrection of his physical body?" To answer all objections, I will address the question from three perspectives: The Deity of the God-man; the Humanity of the God-man; the Incarnation of God with man.

We must examine the deity of the God-man because of questions raised by Physicalism, and because of his intimate union with Jesus of Nazareth. We must examine the humanity of the God-man to show he was a genuine human being, of material body and immaterial soul, conceived in a genuine human being of material body and immaterial soul (by supra-natural means), in the lineage of a genuine human being of material body and immaterial soul, Adam, through his physical descendants, all of material body and immaterial soul, see Luke 3:23–38.

The Deity Of The God-Man

Conditionalism and the Deity of the God-man

Physicalist-Conditionalists do accept the existence of the non-material person God. Their doctrine, whether they will admit to it or not, requires a material God. But God is a unique immaterial spirit being, John 4:24, yet another Scripture doctrine they cannot escape. (Looking to John 4:24. If, as is the case, God must be worshiped in spirit and truth, then the human being created by the Physicalist is incapable of worship, because Physicalism denies human beings have an immaterial spirit with which to worship God.)

Some Physicalist-Conditionalists, recognizing God must be immaterial, distort the orthodox view of the incarnation of God.

> The pre-existent non-material person (God the Son) could become human.
> [http://www.rightreason.org/2012/physicalism-and-the-incarnation/]

This doctrine is not the immaterial God the Son joined in union with a material human being, but that the immaterial God literally set aside his deity and literally became a physical human being.

> God the Son "became a human soul when he was embodied" or "Christ was composed of a human soul and a human body."
> [http://www.rightreason.org/2012/physicalism-and-the-incarnation/]

Again, the doctrine is the immaterial God literally became a material being with a material soul and material body. Remember, in Physicalism there is no actual soul, merely a biological effect. Do not be confused by the sound of words. The Physicalist cannot avoid the use of the term "soul," but their doctrine denies the existence of a soul, so it is dishonest for the Physicalist-Conditionalist to say God the Son "became a human soul when he was embodied."

> Even though God the Son became a material object, he still had properties essential to God. [Lim, article.]

In the particular view of some Physicalist-Conditionalist, God the Son became human but retained his deity powers. Mortals with deity powers sounds familiar, and pagan. Other Physicalist-Conditionalist say God added human nature to his deity. Neither view is scriptural.

The Conditionalist's variety of views of the incarnation are not the biblical view. God the Son did not become human, God the Son did not add humanity to his deity. The biblical view is God the Son joined in union with a genuine human body and a genuine rational human soul. A union is the joining of dissimilar substances. The hammer in my tool box is a union of metal with wood. The metal remains metal, the wood remains wood. God the Son did not *add* humanity *to* his deity, implying an amalgamation, God the Son joined *with* a human being, indicating an indissoluble union of dissimilar things.

In the union that is the incarnation, the deity remained fully genuine deity, the humanity remained fully genuine human. The humanity was not exalted to deity; the deity was not adulterated by humanity. In the union of God the Son with Jesus of Nazareth, no aspect of deity was added to the humanity, and no aspect of humanity was added to the deity.

God the Son joined in union with the human being Jesus of Nazareth, a union that did not change the essence or attributes of either nature. The deity worked through the humanity, the deity did not become human, the deity nature did not exalt the humanity to deity. The statement (creed, definition) of Chalcedon (AD 451) clearly states the biblical view. The incarnate person was:

> truly God and truly man, of a reasonable [rational] soul and body; consubstantial [co-essential] with the Father according to the Godhead, and consubstantial with us according to the Manhood . . ..
>
> one and the same Christ, Son, Lord, only begotten, to

be acknowledged in two natures, inconfusedly, unchangeably, indivisibly, inseparably; the distinction of natures being by no means taken away by the union, but rather the property of each nature being preserved, and concurring in one Person and one Subsistence, not parted or divided into two persons, but one and the same Son, and only begotten, God the Word, the Lord Jesus Christ [Schaff, *Creeds*, 2:62].

Notice in AD 451 the essential, historic, orthodox doctrine of genuine Christianity is Jesus of Nazareth "truly man" possessing a reasonable [rational] soul. Not a soul artificially produced by biological processes, but a "reasonable soul."

Jesus the Christ was "truly God and truly man." God the Son did not become human in the incarnation. Some Physicalists believe "that God the Son became man in the person of Jesus, and that he was and is one person with a human nature and a divine nature" [Lim, article]. He "became man," so therefore did not have a deity nature, but a "divine nature."

The semantic content of "divine" depends on the context in which the word is used. For example, when 2 Peter 1:4 says, "through which [salvation] have been freely given to us great and precious promises, so that through these things you may become partakers of the divine nature, having escaped the corruption in the world by lust," Peter does not mean believers become deity.

Peter means a believer's human nature, that through salvation has been restored to the image and likeness of God, through that quality of life, eternal life, bestowed on the saved. Or as Peter said in 1:3, "his [God's] divine power has given to us [the believer] all things needed for life and godliness." The "divine power of God," are those communicable aspects of his deity nature given to believers that they may possess "all things needed for life and godliness."

As I said before, eternal life is both the duration of life and quality of life God gives to the saved. The duration is endless, forever. The quality is God sharing his communicable attributes in a measure suitable to a finite being, so the believer is conformed to the likeness of Jesus Christ. That is the deity nature communicating the divine nature to the saved.

Therefore, just because someone says Jesus Christ is divine, does not necessarily reflect a belief Jesus the Christ is genuinely deity and genuinely human. Lim, quoted above, is a Physicalist: the Christ might be divine, but he is not deity, because the Physicalist says when deity joined with humanity deity became human.

The Scripture teaches the God-man was one person, with one personality, that of God the Son, with two natures, deity and human, informing the one personality. Scripture does not teach God the Son become man in the incarnation. In the incarnation God the Son continued as unadulterated deity. The Physicalist-Conditionlist's error is the consequence of their false premise human life is biological only, not immaterial also. God the Son did not become a human being in the incarnation, God the Son joined himself in union with a human being in the incarnation. God the Son remained as he was before the incarnation: he was, is, and always will be God the Son, just as from the moment of the incarnation he always will be incarnate, both God and man.

The Physicalist-Conditionlist's premise is just this: the thing we imagine to be an independent, unique human person is merely the effect of certain biological processes—neurons and chemicals and electrical impulses—so not actually a person but a byproduct of biological activity. Change the biology change the person; stop the biology annihilate the person. Physicalist-Conditionlist's is a thoroughly materialistic view of humanity as all body, no soul.

In Physicalism-Conditionalism, the "person" Jesus ceased to exist upon the physical death of Jesus Christ—it became a lifeless decomposing corpse: no biological activity, no mental effect, no person. Therefore, the incarnation ceased to exist when Jesus died, and the Christ ceased to exist when Jesus died (the Christ is an office of the God-man, created by the incarnation, Psalm 2:2, 7). And God the Son, who in some way became a material being in the incarnation, according to Physicalism-Conditionalism, also ceased to exist, because in Physicalism there is no person after physical death. Therefore, God ceased to exist, because without God the Son there is no Trinity, and thus no God; at least not the God of scriptural Christianity. Physicalist-Conditionalist honor God with their lips but deny him in their doctrine; and in their heart.

Physicalism-Conditionalism believes in resurrection.

> If the whole person is constituted by the body, not a immaterial soul joined in union with a material body, then the turning of a body into a corpse is essentially the turning of the whole person into a corpse, with their only hope for life again being the resurrection.

[https://rethinkinghell.com/2012/11/03/whatever-death-means-it-supports-conditionalism/]

Again, a warning of the mendacity of Physicalism-Conditionalism. In Physicalism a "whole person" is only a physical, material body. To say that in death the "whole person" is turned into a corpse, as though there was a an actual, independent person in that body, is to hide the fact that in the doctrines of Physicalism the so-called person is an effect, a byproduct, an ephemeral here-today-gone-tomorrow kind of thing that has no independent existence. In Physicalism there is not a "whole person," only a body producing mental effects that are conveniently identified as a "person." Therefore, in Physicalism-Conditionalism, when the body is corpse there is no "whole person" in the grave, just and only a decomposing body.

> If physicalism or soul-sleep are true, then this alone would explain the need for a resurrection because only at a resurrection could the unsaved stand to face God. [https://rethinkinghell.com/2012/07/22/double-jeopardy-why-raise-the-dead-only-to-destroy-them/]

Physicalism-Conditionalism must resurrect the annihilated person, i.e., the body, to judgment because it wants to maintain a veneer of scriptural authority: "and in as much as it awaits for men to die once, then after that judgment," Hebrews 9:27. But in Physicalism-Conditionalism there is no actual person in the biblical sense of material body and immaterial soul. If the "person" was annihilated at physical death, which it must be because the person is only a biological effect, and thus their immortality denied, then did they not "stand to face God" at physical death? Did they not experience judgment at that death?

Yes, in Physicalism-Conditionalism the "person" is annihilated at physical death, even though the body lies moldering in the grave.

One of the issues in dealing with doctrines such as Physicalism-Conditionalism, is they use the terminology of other beliefs to deceive the unwary, and do not say they have redefined those terms (the dishonesty practiced by all cults). That is why I continue to impress on the reader what Physicalism-Conditionalism means when they use commonly defined terms in an uncommon way.

Judgment in Physicalism-Conditionalism is the un-state of non-existence; physical death in Physicalism causes non-existence; therefore when the body dies the "person" has been judged. The Scripture's doctrine is the immaterial immortal unsaved soul is imprisoned in hades until rejoined with the resurrected body for final judgment, Daniel 12:2; Revelation 20:11–15. Take away the immaterial immortal soul, as Physicalism does, and you have to create a false doctrine to satisfy the biblical doctrine of final judgment and punishment.

Indeed, because every person is unsaved during mortal life according to all the sects of Conditionalism, isn't physical death the judgment of God for their unsaved state? Why resurrect the already judged to judge them again? I can understand the Physicalist-Conditionlist's logic in resurrecting the body of the unsaved elect to the salvation of an immortal body. But why does Physicalism resurrect the body of the unsaved non-elect to a second judgment? Because in Scripture the unsaved are subject to the second, endless, death of body and soul, 2:11; 20:6, 14; 21:8.

The Physicalist-Conditionalist must give their doctrine an outward appearance of being biblical; but the substance of their belief is definitely not scriptural. The Scripture does not teach endless annihilation, but endless separation from God, as I will explain later, below, by giving the scriptural definition of death. I will also examine one of their "proofs" for annihilation, where they distort Augustine of Hippo's doctrine of endless punishment for the unsaved.

In the case of God the Son incarnated in Jesus of Nazareth, Physicalist-Conditionalist doctrine teaches at his death on the cross death the "person" was annihilated. Therefore the incarnation was un-made by the dead body. Was the incarnation re-made when Jesus was resurrected? (How about God the Son? Was he re-made?) I could not discover an answer in the writings I consulted. The Rethinking Hell website also does not answer the relationship between Physicalism and the incarnation, either before, during, or after Jesus Christ was physically dead. Truly, they dare not, because the entire house of cards would come tumbling down.

Physicalism-Conditionalism rejects the "traditional dualism" of the Christ having a human soul in a human body—that is, the Scripture teaching God the Son incarnated with a genuine human soul and genuine human body. That is because in the Physicalist view the human "soul" is really the psychological nature of Jesus (but that psychological nature is only an effect of biology), a material human component of the incarnation, not an immaterial component of humankind. As noted earlier, the intangibles of the soul cannot be reduced to tangibility as the byproduct of a physical body: the Physicalist's "person" is not a genuine person. All Physicalists have this in common: there is no immaterial element in human beings—no soul. I will address the Dualists in the next section, The Humanity of the God-man. But first, let us confirm the deity of the God-man, contra the Physicalist-Conditionalist.

To briefly review the Physicalist-Conditionalist's doctrine of the incarnation of God the Son.

> The pre-existent non-material person (God the Son) could become human.
> [http://www.rightreason.org/2012/physicalism-and-the-incarnation/]
>
> God the Son became a human soul when he was embodied" or "Christ was composed of a human soul and a human body.
> [http://www.rightreason.org/2012/physicalism-and-the-incarnation/]
>
> Even though God the Son became a material object, he still had properties essential to God. [Lim, article.]

In the Physicalist-Conditionalist doctrine of the incarnation of God the Son, God became a material being. What does the Scripture say?

We will begin with the biblical doctrine of God. God is increate, a personal being, a substantive entity, a unique spirit essence having life-in-itself (Exodus 3:14; Genesis 1:26; Isaiah 45:22; John 4:24; 5:26), and therefore without beginning or end, eternal, ever-present, all knowing, all powerful, without limits or limitations, never not God.

The biblical doctrine of God is one essence with three personal subsistences. "Each person is co-equal and co-essential with the other persons. God is Father-Son-Spirit. The Father is God, the Son is God, the Holy Spirit is God. The Father is a person, the Son is a person, the Holy Spirit is a person. One Deity essence, three deity persons. God is one God. All that is in God is God" [Quiggle, *Thirty-six*, 15].

Each member of the Trinity is co-essential with the other members. There is one God, one deity essence, not shared among the members of the Trinity, not combined to make a Trinity, but one essence. God Father-Son-Spirit are co-essential. Each has his own particular work to do, but as being co-essential each participates in the work of the others. Scripture examples this aspect of the work of the Trinity. Father, Son, Spirit worked together.

> The creation, Genesis 1:1; Colossians 1:16; Genesis 1:2
>
> The incarnation, Hebrews 10:5; Philippians 2:7; Luke 1:35
>
> The baptism, Matthew 3:16–17; Mark 1:9–11; Luke 3:21–22; John 1:32–34
>
> The propitiation, Isaiah 53:6, 10; Ephesians 5:2; Hebrews 9:14
>
> The resurrection, Romans 6:4; John 10:17; Romans 8:11
>
> The indwelling, 1 Corinthians 6:19; Colossians 1:27; Ephesians 4:6.

"The Son is eternally begotten of the Father, not as an act

of creation, but because it is the nature of the Father to eternally beget the Son, just as it is the Son's nature to be eternally begotten from the Father. The Holy Spirit proceeds from the Father and the Son because it is their nature for the Spirit to eternally proceed from them, as it is the nature of the Spirit to eternally be proceeding from them" [Quiggle, *Thirty-six*, 15].

The Conditionalist doctrinal statement affirms "our Lord Jesus Christ" is "God manifest in the flesh" [https://rethinkinghell.com/statement/]. Not God become flesh (as in Physicalism), but God revealed (manifest) in flesh. However, within the Conditionalism camp, Physicalists define "God manifest in the flesh" as God becoming fully human in the incarnation. That is what Evangelical Conditionalism, (or at least one of their sects) means by "Jesus Christ is God manifest in the flesh."

There is a seldom thought of aspect of the God-man that affirms he was genuine deity in genuine humanity. That aspect is the consequence of the dual nature of Christ as one person with two natures. William Ames stated it clearly.

> There were in Christ two kinds of understanding: a divine understanding whereby he knew all things, John 21:17, and a human whereby he did not yet know some things, Mark 13:32. So there were two wills, one divine, Luke 5:13, and the other human, with a natural appetite, Matthew 26:39. So Christ has a double presence, but the human presence cannot be everywhere or in many places at once. [Ames, 131].

The one person Jesus Christ was always omnipresent and

localized at one and the same time. The deity nature remained deity, and therefore was omnipresent, an attribute of the person God the Son. The human nature remained human, and therefore was in one place in space and time, an attribute of human nature. [Below from Quiggle, *Biblical Essays IV*, 312.]

> The person Jesus Christ is both eternal (his deity) and immortal (his human soul upon conception, his human body at resurrection).
>
> The person Jesus Christ is both omniscient (his deity) and limited in knowledge and understanding (his humanity).
>
> The person Jesus Christ is both omnipotent (his deity) and limited in ability (his humanity).

The fact of the incarnation is established by Scripture, and held by the Conditionalist, even by the Physicalists within the Conditionalist camp. To the question whether deity continued to be deity in the incarnation, or continued to be deity after Jesus died, Conditionalism gives an inconsistent answer. Some Physicalist-Conditionalists would say yes, others no. Those Dualists-Conditionalists who believe the soul when separated from the body lacks consciousness also cannot give a consistent answer. Did Jesus sleep through physical death until resurrected?

Here are the biblical answers.

> Did the incarnation continue after Jesus Christ died? The Bible answers "Yes."
>
> Did God the Son continue to be God the Son after Jesus Christ died? The Bible answers "Yes."

> Did the human soul of the God-man continue in conscious, active existence after Jesus Christ died? The Bible answers "Yes."

We can confidently answer "Yes," because the incarnation is not about two persons, it is not about two natures, but is all about one person, the one person with two natures who is the God-man. The Scripture always presents Jesus the Christ as one person with one personality, that of God the Son, as informed by his two natures, deity and human. One person whose two natures are in permanent harmonious union.

Philippians 2:5–8 conclusively proves in the incarnation God the Son did not become human, did not become a human soul, did not become a material object, as the Physicalist-Conditionalist supposes. A complete exposition of that passage is well beyond both the scope of this chapter [see Quiggle, *Philippians*]. A few key words will have to suffice.

In 2:6, the word variously translated robbery, advantage, or grasped is *harpagmós*. The idea of *harpagmós* is not robbery, specifically, but taking advantage. "In every instance this idiomatic expression refers to something already present and at one's disposal. The question ... is not whether one possesses something, but whether or not one chooses to exploit something" [O'Brien, 215].

> Christ did not regard the advantage of his deity as grounds to avoid the incarnation; on the contrary, he was willing to regard himself as nothing by taking on human form. Then he further lowered himself in servanthood by obeying God to the point of ignominious

death. [Silva, *Philippians*, 99.]

The word "form" in 2:6 is *morphḗ*. The grammar makes plain that existing in the *morphḗ* of God includes being equal with God: "form of God" is in parallel with "equal with God." "Precisely because he was in the form of God he did not regard this equality with God as something to be used for his own advantage" [O'Brien 216]. Jesus' claim of equality with God could not be *harpagmós* because he truly was equal with God. The expression of his deity in 2:6 is just the same as the expression of his human nature in 2:7—to be in the *morphḗ* of a servant includes being in the likeness of men. He was genuinely God and genuinely human.

In 2:7, the word variously translated "no reputation, emptied, made himself nothing" is *kenóō* which means to make empty. Since he was equal with God, *kenóō* cannot mean he emptied himself of any attribute of his deity, because the unity and simplicity of God means the attributes of deity are inseparable from the essence of deity.

What kind of God would God be if he chose to put off and on at will those specific qualities which make him the being we call 'God'? God has no parts. All that is within God is God. The Son emptied himself of any *outward* appearance of deity, which is to say that in becoming incarnate he did not bring with him any of those outward things by which deity may be recognized by angels and human beings. However, all that is God continued in the incarnation.

The words *morphḗ*, *homoíōma*, and *schḗma* appear in the phrases,

> existing in the essential nature [*morphḗ*] of God ...

having taken taking on his own initiative and power [*lambánō*] the essential nature [*morphḗ*] of a servant ... being in the likeness (*homoíōma*) of men ... having been found in the physical form (*schḗma*) of men.

The Greek words *morphḗ, homoíōma*, and *schḗma* are synonyms. Like all synonyms they are similar in meaning but not identical. The word *morphḗ* means form or substance, essence. Unlike *schḗma*, which deals with the external form, *morphḗ* expresses the inner essentials. In the first use, Jesus was in the *morphḗ* of God because he was God. No one could be in the *morphḗ* of God who was not God. "What Paul asserts, then, when he says that Christ Jesus existed in the 'form of God [KJV],' is that he had all those characterizing qualities which make God to be God, the presence of which constitutes God, and in the absence of which God does not exist. He who is 'in the form of God' is God" [Warfield, 255]. Jesus was fully deity (*morphḗ*), fully human (*morphḗ* and *homoíōma*), and in external appearance (*schḗma*) a male human being, without any outward manifestation of his deity nature (*kenóō*).

Putting it all together:

> 5 Let this mindset be in you that was also in Christ Jesus, 6 who existing in the essential nature of God, did not regard equality with God for his own advantage, 7 but emptied himself of all outward manifestation of deity, having taken on his own initiative and power the essential nature of a servant, being in the likeness of men, sin excepted, 8 and having been found in the physical form of men, he humbled himself, becoming

obedient to death, even the death of the cross.

God the Son voluntarily set aside the outward manifestation of deity, and through the exercise of his omnipotent power he made a union of his deity nature with human nature, that he might become human and mortal as well as deity and eternal in order to pay the penalty for the sin of his erring creature man. The Christ must be mortal that he may die as the punishment for sin; the Christ must be deity that he may give limitless merit to his vicarious, propitiatory death.

Thus we see the apostle Paul, and thereby God who inspired the words, denies the Physicalist-Conditionalist doctrine of the incarnation.

To the saved thief on the cross, Jesus said, "Amen, I say to you, today you will be in Paradise with me" (Luke 23:43). Regardless of what one believes "paradise" to be, Jesus said, "You will be in paradise with *me*" (emphasis mine). The "me" Jesus speaks of is the incarnate person: not the deity, not the human, but the one person, the deity-human God-man Jesus the Christ. The "today" Jesus spoke of was that day in which he and the saved thief died. Therefore, during the three days after his death, the God-man Jesus the Christ did not cease to exist at physical death; the incarnation continued.

The Scripture *always* speaks of Jesus the Christ as one person. The actions of the God-man were not performed by the deity nature or the human nature, but by the person. The words spoken by the God-man were not spoken by the deity nature or the human nature, but by the person. The death of Jesus Christ is spoken of as the death of the person, not of the human nature nor the deity nature (1 Corinthians 15:3). The resurrection of the Christ is not spoken of as the resurrection of the human Jesus, but of the person, the God-man, Jesus Christ (1 Corinthians 15:4, 20). The person slept and the person stilled the storm. The person was hungry and the person created bread in his hands. Scripture does not divide the person. The Christ's works were not performed by the human nature or by the deity nature but by the person expressing himself through the union of his two natures working together in harmony.

What was not divided in life was not divided in death. Because God is the origin and source of all life, God the Son endlessly gives life to that immortal human soul into which he incarnated, even as he does for all human souls. (I will discuss below why all human souls are naturally immortal.) Throughout physical death, the person Jesus the Christ was a living, conscious human soul, because the deity-human person possesses both eternal life and immortal life (respectively). Two things are clear:

> The person Jesus Christ when viewed as the God-man could not die in his deity and humanity and cease to exist as the God-man. That would be a division in the Trinity.
>
> The person Jesus Christ viewed in his humanity could not have died and ceased in his human consciousness while his deity remained intact. That would be a division of the God-man and violate the union formed by the incarnation. (These two points were suggested by a friend, Pastor Brannon Poore.)

God remained God when God joined in union with a human

soul. When the human body of Jesus Christ physically died, God continued to be God; the human being Jesus continued to be Jesus in union with God the Son; the incarnate God-Man continued to be the incarnate God-man. He continued to have a dual presence in the universe: the omnipotent, omniscient, omnipresent God and the limited, finite human soul to which he had joined himself in the permanent union that is the incarnation.

Below, in the section, The Humanity of the God-man, I will demonstrate the Scripture teaches human beings are the union of an immortal immaterial human soul with a mortal material human body: that union of human body and human soul is the humanity with which God the Son joined himself in the permanent union that is the incarnation.

The Humanity Of The God-Man

Introduction

The incarnation of God with man is essential, it is critical, to a proper understanding of the redemption of sinners. The means of redemption designed by God required a human payment for the crime of sin and the limitless merit of deity to propitiate God's holiness and justice for the crime of sin. Limitless merit is a quality possessed by deity alone. A human payment requires two things: human mortality (Hebrews 2:9, 14), and a nature that is the same as the human nature that committed the crime (Hebrews 2:17; 10:4, 10), which means the immaterial soul. The body does not sin, the body is an instrument for acts of sinning, Romans 6:12–13. In this world, during this mortal life, the immaterial human soul is in union with the material body. Therefore God satisfied his requirements to propitiate himself for human sin by joining himself in union with a human being: the incarnation made in human body and human soul.

Before continuing, let me discuss again an important word I used repeatedly in the last section, and will continue to use. That word is "union." A union is when dissimilar things are joined together. Man is a union of immaterial soul joined with material body. The soul itself is a union of dissimilar parts (see below), as is the body, each part functioning together to make those parts into a unified whole: a union, not a unity. A union has parts. God is not a union, God is a unity, because God does not have parts. God's essence has no parts. The Trinity of persons is one essence. God's attributes are not parts of God. The whole essence is in each attribute and each attribute is the whole essence [Shedd, *Dogmatic*, 1:254]. The incarnation of God the Son with Jesus of Nazareth is a union of dissimilar parts: deity and human.

The question, "Was Jesus God?" is of the utmost importance to the redemption of sinners. No, Jesus was and is human, Luke 1:31. Jesus Christ is the God-man, the union of humanity and deity. The insistent theology of modern Christians that "Jesus is God" denies the mortality of the humanity of Jesus the God-man, a mortality that is one of the two *sine qua non* for the redemption of sinners. The propitiation of sin requires a death, Romans 6:23; 3:25a, the death of both body and soul. (I will explain the biblical views of death, further below.)

Jesus of Nazareth was the human component of the incarnate Person who was and is Jesus the Christ, the God-man, the Son of God (a Scripture title that always identifies the incarnate person). God the Son is increate and preexisted Jesus the human being. Jesus the human being was and is a created being. A created being is a person who has a beginning. Scripture demonstrates Jesus the human being had a beginning.

> Luke 1:26–27, 30–31, 34–35, 38, Now, in the sixth month, Gabriel the messenger was sent by God to a city of Galilee, whose name was Nazareth, to a virgin betrothed to a man, whose name was Joseph, of the house of David; and the virgin's name was Mariam. ... And the messenger said to her, "Do not fear Mariam. For you have found favor with God. Look now, you will conceive in your womb, and will bear a son, and you will call his name 'Jesus.' ... Then said Mariam to the messenger, "How will this be, since I know not a man?" And responding the messenger said to her, "The Holy Spirit will come upon you, and the power of Most High will rest upon you. Therefore also the holy begotten will be called, 'Son of God.' ... Then Mariam said, "See the handmaid of the Lord. May it be according to your word." And the messenger departed from her.
>
> Matthew 1:18–21, Now of Jesus Christ the genealogy was in this manner. Mary his mother was betrothed to Joseph. Before they came together, she was pregnant from the Holy Spirit. But Joseph her husband, being righteous, and not willing to expose her publicly, desired to secretly divorce her. But these things he having thought (his spirit was agitated), behold, a messenger of the Lord in a dream appeared to him, saying, "Joseph, son of David, do not fear to receive Mary as your wife, for that conceived in her is from the

Holy Spirit. She will bear a son, and you will call his name Jesus; for he will save his people from their sins."

Another characteristic of some created beings is physical mortality. Not all created beings possess mortality, e.g., the angels, being created as spirit beings, have a beginning, but not mortality. But one characteristic of the created being "humankind" is physical mortality, Genesis 2:17; the repeated "and he died" in Genesis 5; Hebrews 2:9. Jesus, the human component of the incarnate God-man, possessed the human characteristic mortality.

> Hebrews 2:9, 14, Who, however, this one, we see having been made a little lower than the angels, Jesus, through the suffering of death, having been crowned with glory and honor, so that by God's grace he might for all taste death. ... Since, therefore, the children have partaken of blood and of flesh also, he in like manner shared in the same things, so that through death he might render ineffective the one holding the power of death, that is, the Devil.
>
> ^{Jn} Therefore, when Jesus took the vinegar, ^{Mt} again having cried out with a loud voice, ^{Jn} he said, "It is finished. ^{Lu} "Father, into your hands I commit my spirit." ^{Jn} And having bowed his head, ^{Lu} he breathed his last, ^{Jn} he yielded up his spirit. [Quiggle, *Four Voices*, 212.]

The conclusion Scripture leads us to is just this: Jesus of Nazareth, the human component in the incarnate Person, was a created being possessing physical mortality. Jesus the human being was not God. The incarnate God the Son is God, who through incarnation with the human being Jesus of Nazareth became the God-man, Jesus the Christ, the one person, the only person, who could effect redemption, being human and mortal, and deity. Jesus Christ is the God-man, God in union with man, and only in the context of that union of deity with humanity may we say the person Jesus is God. Therefore, more properly, Jesus Christ is God and man.

The deity-human union that is Jesus the Christ satisfied God's requirements for human beings to be redeemed from the crime of their sins. To deny these facts, to make Jesus any kind of god (Mormonism, Buddhism) or only God and not the God-man, (many modern Christians) is denying the humanity and mortality essential to his propitiation of God for sin. It is to deny God's redemptive process, and ultimately to deny our redemption. The God-man must be human to die in order to propitiate God for sin; the God-man must be deity in order to propitiate God for sin: the humanity for death, the deity to give limitless merit to that death.

Jesus the Christ is the God-man, the permanent union of deity and humanity in one person. Jesus Christ is both God and man. Physicalism denies the redemptive power of Jesus Christ by making God the Son become a human being in the incarnation.

Both the human and deity components of the incarnation are essential to redemption. I have previously discussed the deity: God the Son remained God in the incarnation. What, then, are the characteristics of the created being "humankind." More to the point of this discussion, do human beings possess a living, active consciousness that survives the mortality of the body? If the answer from Scripture is, "Yes," then the human component of the incarnate person Jesus Christ was living, conscious, and active during the time his physical body was lying dead in the grave.

This section on the "Humanity of the God-man" will demonstrate the created human being Jesus of Nazareth was a being of material body and immaterial soul, whose soul continued in conscious, active life after the physical death of his body, and that his body was restored to life by the deity-human person Jesus Christ rejoining his human body through resurrection.

Resurrection

Deity is always living, conscious, and active. Was the human consciousness of Jesus Christ living, conscious, and active during the time the physical body was in the grave? How do we know any human being—we have proven from Scripture Jesus of Nazareth was a human being—is living and active and conscious between physical death and physical resurrection?

It is not within the scope of this chapter to defend the resurrection of the physical bodies of the saved and unsaved. All sects of Conditionalism agree all human beings will experience resurrection. However, it is in the interests of this chapter's purpose to explain the manner in which the physically dead body is restored to life in resurrection. That explanation is essential to answering our question concerning the state of the Christ between his death and resurrection, and is absolutely contrary to the doctrines of Physicalist-Conditionalism (no soul) and Substance Dualism-Conditionalism (an unconscious soul during physical death). To that end, a brief review of resurrection is appropriate.

The physical death of the material body, and the resurrection of that same material body, with the restoration of life to that resurrected body, are clearly taught by Scripture. Almost the whole of 1 Corinthians 15 is an exposition of resurrection from the dead. A few scriptures from that passage.

> 1 Corinthians 15:12–13, Now if Christ is proclaimed, that he has been raised out from dead ones, how say some among you that there is not a resurrection of dead ones? But if there is not a resurrection of dead ones, neither has Christ been raised.
>
> 1 Corinthians 15:20, But now Christ has been raised out from dead ones, firstfruit of those becoming asleep.
>
> 1 Corinthians 15:22–23, For as in Adam all die, so also in Christ all will be made alive. But each in their own order: *the* firstfruit Christ, then those of Christ at his coming.
>
> 1 Corinthians 15:42, And in this manner the resurrection of the dead ones. It is sown in decay, it is raised in incorruption.
>
> 1 Corinthians 15:53, For it is necessary this the corruptible to put on incorruption, and this the mortal to put on immortality.

The Old Testament believers will be resurrected. Daniel 12:2, "Many sleeping in the dust of the earth will awake: some to everlasting life, others to reproach and everlasting abhorrence."

The New Testament believers will be resurrected, 1 Thessalonians 4:13–17.

> Now we do not want you to be ignorant, brethren, about those having fallen asleep, so that you should not be grieved, even just as the rest—those not having hope. Because if we believe that Jesus died and rose again, so also God will bring with him those having fallen asleep through Jesus.
>
> For this we declare to you by the word of the Lord, that we the living remaining unto the coming of the Lord, shall never no never precede those having fallen asleep. Because the Lord himself, by a loud command, by the voice of an archangel, and by the trumpet of God, will descend from heaven, and the dead in Christ will rise first. Then we the living remaining, together with them, will be caught up in the clouds for the meeting of the Lord in the air. And so always with the Lord we will be.

All the martyred Tribulation believers will be resurrected. Revelation 20:4, 5, "And I saw thrones, and they sat upon them ... This is the first resurrection."

All the unsaved dead will be resurrected. Revelation 20:6, 12, 13, "Blessed and holy the one having part in the first resurrection. Over these the second death has no power ... And I saw the dead, great and small, standing before the throne ... And the sea gave the dead the ones in it. And Death and hades gave the dead, the ones in them."

Are souls sleeping when the body is dead? "Asleep" is a figure of speech, a biblical euphemism for physical death. The physical death of a believer is not fear-inspiring, but as natural as falling sleep. The body is said to "sleep" because it will be "awakened" at the resurrection. The physically dead believer, i.e., the immortal soul—the soul is the person—is living, conscious, and active because "God will bring with him those having fallen asleep [physically died] through Jesus."

The false doctrine of the Conditionalist-Substance Dualists is the soul sleeps until resurrected. If, as is the case, God is bringing with him those who have physically died, for the purpose of restoring them to their resurrected bodies, then those who have "fallen asleep through Jesus" are living, and conscious, and active in heaven with Jesus, and only physically dead.

We have two clear instances in Scripture of an un-resurrected, physically dead person being alive, conscious, and active between physical death and resurrection. The first is the prophet Samuel, 1 Samuel 28:11–19. If we believe the Scripture always gives an accurate, authentic, and credible report of historical events (inspiration and inerrancy), then we must believe God allowed Samuel to appear to Saul after Samuel's physical death but before Samuel's resurrection. The second is Moses the Law-giver, Matthew 17:1–3, clearly an instance of a living, conscious, active person between physical death (Deuteronomy 34:5–6) and resurrection. Both these instances deny the doctrines of Physicalism and Substance Dualism.

(One might think of Elijah as an example, Matthew 17:1–3, and I believe he was. However, Elijah was taken into heaven by a "chariot of fire," 2 Kings 2:11, which might be considered a translation into heaven [taken alive into heaven] not a transition into heaven through physical death.)

The soul does not sleep "in the dust of the earth," the body "sleeps in the dust of the earth," Genesis 3:19, until resurrection. In Genesis 2:7 God formed Adam's physical body from the dust of the earth, and "breathed" the soul into the inert body. The body was taken out of the ground and to the ground it would return, Genesis 3:19. "Man's spirit departs, he returns to his earth," Psalm 146:4, and the soul returns to God who made it, "all souls are mine," Ezekiel 18:4.

As I have shown through the examples of Samuel and Moses (and possibly Elijah), the person is actively conscious, the body "sleeps" in physical death.

Resurrection is, "The reuniting of an individual soul with its original body after physical death has occurred. Resurrection encompasses two processes: 1) God reforms the physically dead body from existing materials and, 2) God causes the disembodied soul originally propagated with that body to unite with it and animate it. The united soul and resurrected body will continue in that reunited state throughout eternity." [Quiggle, *Dictionary*, s. v. Resurrection.]

When the body of the saved person is resurrected, it is reformed free from the presence of sin and transformed and glorified to be eternally incorruptible (1 Corinthians 15:50). Then the saved, immortal, incorruptible soul is rejoined to the resurrected immortal, incorruptible body to animate the body. The saved live eternally in the state of reunited immortal body and immortal soul without sin or corruption.

In the unsaved, resurrection reunites a sinful immortal

corrupted soul with a sinful and corrupted body made immortal to endure judgment and endless punishment.

Based on the above scriptures (and others) all accept the fact physical resurrection to life out of physical death is proven by the scriptures for every human being. The following discussion will show how the non-living resurrected body is returned to the state of "alive" by God rejoining the soul to the body.

Life

Physical death is when the state of the material body changes from "alive" to an inert, non-living, lump of decomposing dirt (Genesis 2:7, the body was formed from the "dust of the ground"). Physical resurrection is when God re-forms the original body from its decomposed state and restores that body to the state of physical life.

The essential question is, in what manner does God restore the physically dead resurrected body to physical life. We begin an answer with another question: What is life?

We—the "we" that is humankind—define life by its effects not by its essence; so does the Bible. Human beings are designed for the immaterial soul to function through the material body. During this mortal life, the perceptions available to the soul are limited by the mortal body, in that the body has no mental or visual perception of the immaterial things of the spirit domain (unless such perception is temporarily given by the Holy Spirit, e.g., 2 Kings 6:17). That which we call "life" is an immaterial essence, and therefore not knowable as itself but known only by its affects in the material domain. (Which is why the physical sciences cannot detect the immaterial soul.)

We recognize life by its works, because we are not able to comprehend its essence. What the Bible calls "life" is an immaterial essence created by God *ex nihilo* (from nothing). God himself has life in himself—he is self-existent: *hāyâ ʽāsher hāyâ,* "I am he who exists," Exodus 3:14; John 5:26, and therefore God is increate. God is the origin and source of the life within all living beings, because only God has life in himself.

At the beginning the Bible teaches God is the origin and source of human life. At Genesis 2:7, God formed a human body from dirt, created the human essence from nothing, and placed the immaterial essence "life" and the immaterial human essence "soul" into the non-living human body, thereby enlivening the non-living body, with the result, *'ādām* ["man," in the sense of humankind, and specifically this one man] became a living person.

From this scripture it should be apparent the immaterial essence which we (and the Scripture) identify as "life" is independent of the material body. The material body was formed out of existing non-living material things, then the immaterial essence life was placed in the body along with the human essence God created *ex nihilo*. The body existed as an inert, non-living, non-functional material form; the essence life, of which God alone is the origin and source, was separate from the body; God placed the essence life into the material body, thereby animating the material body: the immaterial essence life made the material body alive. The union of non-living material body and immaterial life plus human essence created a fully functional human being: Adam. "Life" is the animating principle.

The Scripture, in fact, says more happened than the animation of the material body. When the essence life and the human essence was placed into the non-living body, at that moment Adam became "a living person." The word I have translated "person" is the Hebrew *nepesh* [Harris, et al., s. v. 1395a]. In relation to human beings, *nepesh* means "person," ("he is a living person" [Hamilton, 159]). In scripture contexts where *nepesh* refers to a human being, the word is rightly translated "soul" or "person."

The non-living material body became part of a person when the independently existing immaterial soul was placed in the body. In Genesis 2:7, "person" refers to the two parts, material body and immaterial soul, in union, and that is how the Hebrew and Greek words for person or soul are used in Scripture, the union of the immaterial soul and material body.

The Bible usually speaks phenomenally, not scientifically, not technically. The observed phenomenon is a physically living person. The issue is not that Adam became a living being, but why he became a living being. Adam became a living being because the immaterial person Adam, whom God created *ex nihilo,* and the essence "life," were joined in union with the non-living material body, thereby forming a living being from a phenomenal point of view.

All human life is propagated from this one human being. He is not the origin and source of life (God alone is the origin and source), but Adam is the conduit through which all human beings receive life, through those biological processes, established by God, by which life is transmitted from parents to child. Adam is the original, every other human being, including Eve, including Mary, including Jesus of Mary, is a product of the life given to Adam.

That Adam and the Woman (Eve) transmitted a physical body to their offspring is obvious: Cain, Abel, Seth, sons and daughters. Equally obvious is Adam and Eve's offspring transmitted a physical body to their offspring. Adam, Eve, and their offspring all also transmitted a soul to their offspring. How?

A zygote (the fertilized ovum) is a physical thing: a specialized living human cell. All that the zygote is at conception is what develops into the human being we see at birth. The zygote is human, nothing is added during the nine months in the womb to make it human, because he or she begins as human.

Genesis 4:1–2 implies as much, and Genesis 5:3 says it clearly, "Adam reproduced in his own image and likeness." Because Adam, with Eve, propagated others in their image and likeness, that image and likeness was not merely a physical body but also a *nepesh*, a soul, a person. The same kind of immaterial human soul that God placed in Adam and formed in Eve from Adam's soul.

God's Law of Biological Reproduction is each living thing reproduces according to its own kind, and no other kind. We see this law in action every day. There are about 10,000 species of birds, but they all have this in common: they are of the same kind, bird. Human beings reproduce more human beings and only human beings. Adam and Eve, as beings of an immaterial *nepesh*, a soul, which is in union with a material body, reproduced their kind: human beings of immaterial soul in union with material body.

Exactly how a new soul is transmitted from parents to child is a process of the spirit domain, and therefore the exact manner cannot be known. But we are able to draw a reasonable understanding from what we do know about reproduction.

The two gametes—sperm and ovum—are specialized living cells. The essence "life" is part of the composition of every living cell, else a cell would not be alive. The essence "life" is a component of the *nepesh*, the soul, which is the person (I will explain below). The manner in which the body and soul are connected cannot be known, but we might say the body is saturated with the soul. An illustration: when a washcloth is saturated with water, the water is everywhere in the cloth, but the two substances remain distinct. So the human soul in the human body. The immaterial soul in union with the material body is defined in time and space by the location of that material body in time and space. But as an immaterial essence, the whole soul is present everywhere in the body.

The specialized cells for reproduction are not different in this than non-specialized cells: they are saturated with the presence of the soul. But as being specialized for reproduction, they are in some manner capable of communicating the immaterial parts necessary to form a new, never-before-existing soul, at the same time as they communicate the material parts necessary to form a new, never-before-existing body. The soul of the mother in the ovum merges with—we cannot say how—the soul of the father in the sperm to create a new soul. A more mechanistic, a more biological, a more than that brief attempt to define the process we cannot say. The danger in further attempts to understand that wholly immaterial process by which a new soul is created is to reduce the immaterial to the biological—to Physicalism.

When the living cells combine—when the sperm fertilizes the ovum—what is formed is not the immaterial essence life, but life communicated by the male and female gametes to an individual human person who has been formed body and soul through the combination of the material and immaterial parts transmitted by the parents in the gametes. More simply, human persons reproduce more human persons: God's Law of Biological Reproduction at work.

From the moment of fertilization—the moment of conception—the fertilized ovum (a zygote) is a human being: a living human soul in union with a human body made alive by the life in the soul: a human person. The newly conceived person is rudimentary in physical form and incomplex in soul, but nonetheless a human being in body and soul. The fully developed body and soul one sees at birth began with the rudimentary body and soul of the zygote at conception—for nothing is added to the zygote as it develops in the womb, except nourishment from the mother. All that a human being is from conception to physical death (at any age) was present in the gametes of the mother and father, and therefore present in the zygote that is the result of the union of the gametes at conception. At conception, a new human person is formed, body and soul.

Body and soul mature together throughout the life span of the individual. A lifespan begins at the individual's conception and ends at the termination of his or her physical life. At the end of physical life the human person, the soul, continues living—the human soul is in union with the human body, Genesis 2:7, it is not in unity with the human body—because the animating principle "life" is in the soul. Every human being, including Eve, including Mary, including Jesus born of Mary, is a product of the life given to Adam: Eve was formed (not created as was Adam) body and soul from Adam's body and soul; the rest us were propagated through Adam's procreation with Eve. (This understanding is the basis for the doctrine of Traducianism: the physical body and the individual soul containing the attribute sin are transmitted from parents to child [Harrison, s. v. Traducianism], beginning with Adam and Eve; Paul's argument in Romans 5:12.)

From this event at Genesis 2:7, we may derive a usable definition of the immaterial essence "life."

> Life is an immaterial spirit essence originating in God that when placed into non-living physical material causes that non-living material to possess the qualities we recognize and describe as alive.

Human Life

A human life is more than being alive. Human life is the sum of all those characteristics we define as a human being. A human being is not merely alive, but possesses the human essence and human attributes. Humankind created in God's image, Genesis 1:26–27, is a soul: a person fashioned according to the pattern of God's communicable attributes in finite measure, in a greater or lesser degree, depending on the attribute in question. Those communicable attributes of God reproduced (in finite measure) in his creation humankind are these.

> Moral image: holiness, sanctification, righteousness, justice, mercy, faithfulness.
>
> Intellectual image: personality, will, volition, veracity, knowledge, wisdom.
>
> Spiritual image: love, compassion, goodness, kindness, longsuffering, mercy. [Quiggle, *Incarnate*, 42.]

Not one component of the image of God in humankind is physical. How could it be? God is not a man, he is not a physical, material being. Physicalism says a "person" is the mental effect of certain biological processes. But even Physicalism-Conditionalism is forced to agree God is not a physical being.

The image and likeness of God in which humankind was created is not the physical body, but is the human essence and human nature, which are wholly non-physical, wholly immaterial, not biological. The human person is not the effect of the body's biology but is the consequence of God's creation of the human soul, Genesis 2:7. Thus the material human being we physically see is in truth an immortal immaterial human soul existing in union with the material mortal body, but always existing independent of the body: a union not a unity. All human beings are body and soul, as was Adam, procreated in the image and likeness of the person, Genesis 1:26–27; 2:7, 21–23; 3:20; 4:1–2; 5:3, whom God created as the union of material body and immaterial soul.

Therefore the *nepesh*, the soul, the person Adam whom

God created and placed into the inert, non-living material body, was a person created in God's image and likeness, composed of the animating principle life, the human essence, and the attributes of human nature: in a word, a living, conscious, active soul, a genuine person, created independent of the material body, designed to function in harmony with the material body. As Adam was, all human beings are, for we are all derived from Adam: each kind reproduces its own kind.

Now that we understand physical life is the result of the immaterial soul, the person, as present in the material body, we are able to define physical death: the separation of the person from the physical form. And now having an understanding of life and death, we are able define the means by which "alive" is restored to the non-living resurrected body: the reunion of the immaterial person with the resurrected physical body. By means of that reunion the physical body is once again made alive.

We have come a long way in answering the question, "is a human being living and conscious between physical death and physical resurrection?" We have established the essence "life" that makes the body alive is not only an animating principle, but is an indissoluble part of the person: a thing of spirit, an immaterial essence not a material substance, that with the human essence and human attributes creates a person. The observed biological processes of the body result from the presence of the person in the body; those biological processes are not the source of the person, they are the product of the presence of the person in the body. A person is not a byproduct of a biological process.

Physicalism is a barren, lifeless doctrine: it lacks an immaterial living soul. The *nepesh*, the immaterial soul, which is the person, is not dependent upon the body for its existence, but has existence as an immaterial essence separate and distinct from the body and independent of the body. The body without the soul has no life. The life of the body is dependent on the presence of the person, the soul, in the body. The mind in the body is the immaterial person, the soul, acting through the material body.

Therefore, when the biological processes we think of as "life" stop functioning, a state we recognize as physical death, it is because the person, the human soul—which is the animating source of those biological processes—has separated from the body. As the person is not dependent on the body for its existence—Adam's soul had existence before being placed into the body—the soul, the person, continues to exist and be living and active and conscious when separated from the body. The immaterial essence "life" of an individual person cannot be annihilated once established by the processes of procreation. I will prove that proposition later.

In relation to humankind propagated by Adam and Eve, the qualities of the soul—life, the human essence, and the human attributes of the procreated person—are brought into existence at the formation of the zygote, not as produced by the gametes, but as communicated by the gametes: the immaterial soul occupying its God-designed and designated place in the material body.

Let us return to Genesis. When we examine Adam, we are

immediately struck with the understanding he is more than alive—there is something more than the immaterial essence "life" in that body. An amoeba is alive, the smallest bacteria (mycoplasma genitalium) is alive, a virus is … actually, no one knows if viruses are alive or just a chemical process. But Adam has those qualities we name consciousness and sentience. Adam thinks, Adam is aware of himself, Adam learns, Adam has moral understanding, Adam worships. Adam is a living, self-conscious, sentient being (see Quiggle, *Adam and Eve*). As Adam was, we are, because we are all procreated from Adam.

What was the source of Adam's consciousness and sentience? Our choices are non-living dirt, or the living immaterial essence, the person Adam, a human soul, whom God placed into the body. As to dirt,

> The origin of life is a total mystery, and so is the existence of human consciousness. We have no clear idea how the electrical discharges occurring in nerve cells in our brains are connected with our feelings and desires and actions. [Dyson, 11.]

Dyson didn't know, but blindly he believed the physical creates the immaterial: human consciousness. But we know. Scripture teaches the immaterial person is the consciousness, in union with and acting through the body, via "the electrical discharges occurring in nerve cells in our brains," and "our feelings and desires and actions" that originate in the living immaterial soul.

Obviously, at least to the Christian informed by Scripture, Adam's consciousness and sentience did not come from the non-living dirt; in terms of Physicalism, Adam's consciousness and sentience did not come from the physical body. The conclusion should be equally as obvious; God placed into the inert non-living body something more than the animating principle "life."

When we examine Adam—indeed, when we examine ourselves—we discover Adam had three things in addition to the animating principle: an essence or nature that defined him as a human being not some other kind of living being; human attributes that are the expression of that human essence; and personality, which is the ever-developing synergistic effect of essence, attributes, and environment that defined him as an individual human being. So, also, every human being.

When a person physically dies, those four things—life, human essence, human attributes, and human personality—separate from the physical body because they are the components of the soul; they are the person. The reason they all leave together is because they all came to the physical body together. Just as all the biological processes are within one container, the physical body, even so all the immaterial things of a human being are in one container, which the Bible identifies as (Hebrew) *nepesh*, (Greek), *psuché*, and (English) "soul" or "person."

Returning to Genesis 2:7, the most accurate translation of *nepesh* is, "living person." The word *nepesh* is translated "soul" or "person" most of the 754 times it occurs in the Old Testament. In the New Testament the word is *psuché*, 37 occurrences, indicating the immaterial part of a human being. The way both words are used allows the translation "person" or "self." The soul is the person, because the soul contains all those immaterial elements that compose a person. A person, a soul, consists of the animating principle life, the human essence, human attributes, and a personality that develops as the person develops.

In four words the human soul is life, essence, nature, personality. In two words, the human soul is consciousness and sentience. In one word, the human soul is a person. Human physical, mortal life is the presence of the person in the body; human physical death is the absence of the person from the body; resurrection is the restoration of the person to the body.

The soul, unlike the body, being an immaterial essence of the spirit domain, is not subject to cessation of existence: not subject to death. When the Scripture states, as it does, "The *nepesh* who sins it shall die" (Ezekiel 18:20), it is a general statement in agreement with Romans 6:23, the wages of sin is death: physical death, which is the separation of the soul from the body, and spiritual death, which is the separation of the person from God. But the gift of God is eternal life—not immortal life, which is an intrinsic quality of the soul, but that quality of life given to the saved person by God in Christ, wherein God shares his communicable attributes in a measure suitable to a finite being.

(Eternal life is not the same as immortality. In Scripture, "eternal life" is more than duration of life, e.g., John 17:3. At Romans 6:23 eternal life is contrasted with death both spiritual and physical, and therefore eternal life must be both spiritual life (a quality of life) and physical life. At John 3:15; 10:28 Jesus said everyone to whom he gave eternal life would never perish. But believers do perish: they die; to date every believer has died, or will die unless raptured. Therefore, that eternal life Jesus gives the believer, must be something other than the endless duration of physical life.)

Eternal life is a quality of life God gives the saved during this mortal life that changes them from sinner to saved and regenerates their human nature to born-again. The eternal life of the saved is a quality of life God imparts or adds to the believer at salvation, wherein he shares his communicable attributes in a measure suitable to a finite being, changing them into the image of Christ during this mortal life, Romans 8:29. Eternal life is the "seed" that grows into a life of habitual righteousness in the believer, 1 John 3:9.

The believer's eternal life is endless once received, which is by salvation during this mortal life. The eternal life of the believer endures throughout mortal life, death, and resurrection, always continuing endlessly in the presence of God.

As an aid to understanding, I envision the soul as an immaterial container, in which the immaterial elements life, human essence, and human attributes (and personality as it develops) are enclosed, and thereby having a defined and limited location in the universe in time and space. Therefore, viewing the soul as a container for the essential parts—life, essence, attributes—I understand these parts to be indissolubly joined in a union; that these parts, through that reproductive process of gametes uniting in conception, form a new soul in a new body.

The physical body is not the soul's container, but only one

component of a human being that joined in union with the soul makes the soul (the person) suitable for life in the material domain (and after resurrection suitable for life in both material and spirit domains).

If, as Scripture teaches, the person continues living, conscious, and active after physical death (the examples of Samuel, Moses, and Elijah, Mark 9:4. Compare Luke 16:23. See also Revelation 6:9; 7:13–15), then all persons must continue in some manner of finite limited form strictly defined by time and space after physical death. Only God is omnipresent, only God is unlimited in time and space, only God has no defined form. Immaterial beings, such as the disembodied human soul and the spirit beings angels, must have a limited form, as defined by time and space, which is suitable to their presence in the spirit domain. What to call that defined and limited immaterial form but some kind of container: a "body" suited for life in the spirit domain.

The soul may or may not be an immaterial container holding the immaterial elements that together compose a human person. Those immaterial elements may be joined together in some other manner so as to work together. But they are joined together indissolubly, because together they are the human person. Container or not, Scripture identifies the soul as the person, the presence of the person in the body as physical life, and the absence of the person from the body as physical death.

Because the soul is not the product of the physical body, the soul has a continuing existence after it leaves the body, and a defined presence in the time and space of the spirit domain (in heaven or hades) when separated from the material body. God gave the soul life as an intrinsic component of the soul; therefore the soul, the person, is immortal.

At Genesis 2:7, "man became a living person." We understand a human being is the union of material body and those immaterial elements that together the Scripture calls a "soul." The soul, not the body, is the person. The soul works through the body when in union with the body, but just as the body has a continuing existence without the soul as physical human remains, even so the soul, the person, has continuing existence without the body as an individual in living, active, conscious existence. (A discussion of a location for that existence when apart from then body is beyond the scope of this chapter, but my view is from the days of Adam to the end of the Millennial Kingdom, Revelation 20:11, the two locations are in God's presence or in hades.)

We may settle this question of the independent and immortal existence of the soul easily and scripturally. Scripture recognizes the dissolution of the human body, but there is no known dissolution of the human soul in Scripture. The biblical view is once the person comes into existence, that personal existence continues endlessly. "I am," said God at Exodus 3:15, "the God of Abraham, the God of Isaac, and the God of Jacob"; "He is not," said Jesus, "God of the dead but of the living," Mark 12:27, quoting Exodus 3:15. Physical death means the body becomes non-living, but the person continues living.

There is another term we must discuss: substantive entity. The word "substantive" means "existing independently." An "entity" is a self-contained being with genuine, distinct, independent existence. A human person is an immaterial substantive entity. The elements of a person (life, essence, attributes, personality) are not in and of themselves the person, but synergistically form a person. As Genesis 2:7 has taught us, by showing the creation of the person independent of the body, a person does not require a body to be a person.

(A personality is the sum of the attributes of human nature plus the behavior pattern which results from the decision-making faculty of the nature [the "will"], and is not to be confused with a substantive entity. A personality is not a person, but is part of a person.)

An Immortal Soul

Those Conditionalists who believe in the dualism of material body and immaterial soul teach a "conditional immortality" of the human soul.

> Conditionalism is the view that life is the Creator's provisional gift to all, which will ultimately be granted forever to the saved and revoked forever from the unsaved. [https://rethinkinghell.com/statement/]

> The unsaved will be raised in shame and dishonor, to face God and receive the just condemnation for their sins. When the penalty is carried out, they will be permanently excluded from eternal life by means of a final death, implicating the whole person in a destruction of human life and being (Matthew 10:28). [https://rethinkinghell.com/statement/]

The Conditionalist defends a conditional immortality from

several scriptures, but each defense has in common a misunderstanding of the Greek word *apóllumi* (and the word from which it is derived, *ólethros* [Zodhiates, s. v. 3639], 2 Thessalonians 1:9). It is not necessary to examine every scripture where *apóllumi* or *ólethros* are used. Because the Conditionalist doctrinal statement gives Matthew 10:28 as support, I will examine that scripture. My translation.

> Matthew 10:28, And do not be afraid of those killing [*apokteínō*] the body, but are not able to kill [*apokteínō*] the soul; but fear rather the one being able to ruin [*apóllumi*] both soul and body in Gehenna.

I have translated *apóllumi* as "ruin" because according to the teaching of Scripture as a whole, there is no known physical material cause that is able to put to death the human soul. I say the "teaching of Scripture as a whole" because the whole teaching of Scripture cannot be encapsulated, nor epitomized, nor completely stated in just one verse, which is what Conditionalism tries to do. The teaching of Scripture as a whole must be considered when understanding how the Scripture uses *apóllumi*. I will also examine how first century culture understood and used *apóllumi*.

The person's body may be put to death, but the person, the soul, cannot be put to death by any means available to human beings. God is able to *apóllumi* both soul and body in Gehenna (the lake of fire). What does that mean?

The answer requires us to discern how the word *apóllumi* was used in the secular culture of biblical times, and how the Holy Spirit through his human authors used *apóllumi* in Scripture.

The word occurs ninety-two times in the Textus Receptus, ninety times in the NA27. (The Strong's number is Greek 622; the Goodrick-Kohlenberger number is Greek 660. See Zodhiates, s. v. 622.)

In most uses, *apóllumi* means destroy in the sense of physical death. However, at Matthew 9:17 the word means destroy in the sense of ruin, "Nor do they pour new wine into old wineskins; but if it is the wineskins burst and the wine is spilled and the wineskins *apóllumi:* not annihilated but ruined. At Matthew 15:24 the word means unsaved, "But answering he said, "I was not sent except to the lost (*apóllumi*) sheep of the house of Israel."

The Conditionalist says unsaved persons will cease to exist, *apóllumi*, through their punishment in the lake of fire. What about other immaterial substantive entities? At Mark 1:24 (parallel Luke 4:34) a fallen angel asks Jesus Christ, "What do you have to do with us, Jesus of Nazareth? Are you come to destroy [*apóllumi*] us?" Consistent with their beliefs, the Conditionalists say God causes the fallen angels to cease to exist in the lake of fire.

There is a good reason the Conditionalist doctrinal statement references only Matthew 10:28 as support for their doctrine of the eventual annihilation of the soul. Matthew 10:28 is the only verse that says God will *apóllumi* the soul of the unsaved. In every other use in the New Testament scriptures the meaning in each individual context is clearly ruin or physical death. So too at Matthew 10:28. The *apóllumi* of unsaved human beings and fallen angels in the lake of fire is ruin not annihilation, not the cessation of personal existence, not non-existence.

The biblical use of *apóllumi* is the same as the secular use. Moulton and Milligan example from the papyri: the loss of money, the loss of clothing, the loss of life of two pigs [Moulton, s. v. 622]. Gerhard Kittle shows in Greek secular literature the word was used "to destroy or kill in battle; to suffer loss of money." In other uses, "to trifle away one's life … thereby bringing themselves to destruction" i.e., to ruin [Kittel, 1:394].

We turn to Silva [*NIDNT*, 1:357]. *Apóllumi* was used in Homer of slaughter in war. To "disappear, be lost, be ruined (financially), perish, die … injury, destruction, final end of earthly existence … sickness in body, rot in wood, rust in iron." In a specific theological sense in the New Testament, "definite destruction, not merely in the sense of extinction of physical existence, but rather of an eternal plunge into hades and a hopeless destiny of death … Over against life with God there stands the terrible possibility of eternal perdition." (Eternal: unending; Perdition: a state of endless punishment and damnation into which a sinful and un-penitent person passes after death.)

The use at Matthew 10:28 conforms to all other Scripture uses and all secular uses. *Apóllumi* "is not annihilation, but endless punishment in Gehenna (the real hell)" [Robertson, 1:83]. Looking to the verse in context, "men should fear, i.e., all human beings should reverence-respect-worship God, 10:28, because he can *apóllumi* the soul and the body in hell, i.e., endless punishment in the lake of fire" [Quiggle, *Matthew*, 183]. 'Destroy' is not annihilation (a concept foreign to Scripture) but endless ruin through endless separation from God.

Unbelievers are endlessly separated from God (experiencing only his just wrath) at their physical death, and therefore should reverence God in the here and now (by believing on Christ as their Savior). Believers should not fear physical death because they are in an endless salvific relationship with God in Christ, and therefore should always reverence God and not fear what man may do.

In chapter 1, I answered the question, "How do we know a human being is living between physical death and physical resurrection?" Answer: Genesis 2:7 reveals a person is a self-contained being of life, essence, and attributes with a genuine, distinct, and independent existence apart from the physical body. A person is a substantive entity that has life as an intrinsic component of its existence, that was created *ex nihilo*, independent of the material body, and therefore can exist without the material body. Therefore the person has a continuing existence after leaving the physical body.

Physical death is when the person is absent from the body. Scripture never states the dissolution of the immortal immaterial substantive entity that is a human (or angel) person. The complete absence in Scripture of the annihilation of the soul—the soul is the person—is the complete absence of support for the doctrines of annihilationism.

Is the person conscious during physical death? I have shown Scripture examples of several persons conscious during physical death. In addition, Jesus told the believing thief on the cross that he and Jesus would be, that day, in paradise, Luke

23:43. That is a positive assurance of conscious existence during physical death.

Paul, at 2 Corinthians 5:8, expressed that assurance. "Now we are full of confidence and are pleased, rather, to be absent away from the body and to be at home with the Lord." Paul says he has positive assurance when he dies he will be living, conscious, and active at home with Christ. Paul at a later date, in more dire circumstances, expressed the same confidence at Philippians 1:23, "I am constrained between the two [life, death], having the desire to depart [physically die] and to be with Christ, for that is much better." To "be with Christ," implies a conscious existence after death, for he is, as Jesus said, the God of the living.

Jesus, at Luke 16:23 told us the location immediately after physical death of every non-believer at any time in the history of the world: "and being in torments in hades." To be in torments one must be living a conscious existence. At the ending of this present world (2 Peter 3:10; Revelation 20:11; 21:1), the unsaved person who is in hades will be joined to his or her resurrected body and relocated permanently, endlessly, to the lake of fire, Revelation 20:14, "And Death and Hades were thrown into the lake of fire. This the second death is the lake of fire." There they will experience the endless ruin (*apóllumi*) of body and soul through endless punishment.

Some will say Luke 16:23 doesn't count: it was a parable. But a parable is a true-to-life story. A parable is always constructed from literal things: a banquet; a vineyard, a farmer, a field, servants, sons, etc. The persons Lazarus and Rich Man may have been fictional characters, but they represented genuine human beings, saved and unsaved, respectively. The names of the respective locations, hades and Abraham's Bosom, may have been fictional designations, but they represented literal locations—not earthly locations, but locations in the spirit domain suitable to disembodied souls.

I have shown Scripture teaches the person is an immortal immaterial substantive entity, so the persons in Luke 16 went somewhere suitable to immortal immaterial substantive persons after physical death. (Compare Baruch 2:17, "for the dead, who are in hades, whose breath has been taken from their bodies" [Goodspeed, 333]. Here is evidence, ca. first century BC, of belief in the dual nature of human beings, that life is the result of a spirit [breath] in the body, and of a location for disembodied persons.) Jesus says the rich man, Lazarus, and Abraham were living, conscious, and active after physical death.

A parable is a story—a word picture or an illustration—told to teach a single point. A parable is built with things literal (a farmer sowing seed, a man giving a banquet), but may also use figures of speech, idioms, slang, symbols, or types. A parable is always based in something literal and always teaches something literal. No parable is intended to describe every aspect of doctrine, but only to illustrate one point.

What was the point of the parable of the Rich Man and Lazarus? This one has two points. One, no one escapes hades. If there is no soul, Physicalist-Conditionalism, or if the soul is asleep, Substance Dualist-Conditionalism, then Christ's parable is a fable, a story populated with imaginary characters to make a moral point. What would be the moral point if the parable was actually a fable?

The Rich Man, a genuine person—a disembodied living, active, conscious soul in hades—representing all genuine persons in hades, certainly knew he could not escape, because he asks Abraham to send Lazarus (16:27) as a witness to his brothers, indicating the disembodied Lazarus was living, conscious, and active; the Rich Man was asking for a resurrection. Therein hangs the second point: even if a formerly-dead-now-resurrected person testified, they would not believe. Conclusion: there is nothing in this parable that prevents living conscious activity after death for all unsaved. The parable assumes, and thereby teaches, that living conscious activity after death is the normal state of the physically dead. If no unsaved person is able to escape hades, then all in hades are present as living, conscious, active persons.

A person, saved or unsaved, is living, conscious, and active between physical death and physical resurrection—and beyond, endlessly. Regardless of where one believes the person Jesus Christ went after his body physically died [see Quiggle, *Did Jesus Go to Hell?*], the human soul of Jesus Christ was living, conscious, and active after his physical life ended. One, because his human soul is indissolubly in union with God the Son; two, because the human soul is an immaterial substantive entity, of which life is a constituent component, and therefore has immortality.

I demonstrated in the first section the God-man was deity as well as human. Deity cannot cease being deity; deity cannot die; deity cannot stop existing. Deity is always living, conscious, and active. This deity person of the Trinity, God the Son, is permanently in union with the human soul of Jesus, supplying the personality of the God-man, and by that union possessing both human consciousness and deity consciousness, thus continuing consciousness throughout life, physical death, resurrection, and endlessly thereafter.

Therefore Jesus the Christ was living, conscious, and active after his physical life ended—the human consciousness and the deity consciousness were both living and active. God the Son was and is the personality of the God-man, his consciousness was and is the blending of human and deity consciousness. God does not sleep (Psalm 121:3–4), God does not die (John 5:26), so the deity consciousness was always living and active. Human consciousness is always active, even in physical sleep, even in brain death. The "brain death" of the person with traumatic injuries to the physical brain is an indication the soul is no longer interacting through the physical brain: the soul has separated from the body. The fact the "brain dead" body is being kept physically functioning by artificial means simply proves the point. The consciousness, the soul, the person continues living and active after leaving the body.

Excursus: Two Wills

In the above paragraph I say the consciousness of the deity nature and the consciousness of the human nature—both functions of the deity essence and the human essence—blended. I use "blended" in the same sense Charles Ryrie used it when discussing the two wills of Jesus Christ [the "will" is a function of the nature: it is the decision-making faculty]. Ryrie said, "The single person of the incarnate Christ retained the total complex of divine attributes and possessed all the complex of human attributes essential to a perfect human being"

[Ryrie, *Basic*, 287–288]. He then asked, "Did Christ have two wills?" He answered, "It seems to me that every single decision stemmed from either the 'will' of His divine nature or the 'will' of His human nature or a blending of both, making it proper to think of two 'wills'" [Ryrie, *Basic*, 289].

Each nature supplied consciousness to the God-man. No matter how difficult to comprehend, it is the inevitable consequence of possessing two natures. The most rational way to comprehend is to accept a blending of the two; not merging, but blending, retaining the separateness of the deity and human natures. Oil and water may be blended into a union, but cannot merge into a unity. So also the human and deity natures blended into a union.

Returning to the argument

The Son of God, the incarnate person, was conscious between his physical death and resurrection, because of the human consciousness and deity consciousness of the incarnate person.

At John 5:17, Jesus said, "My Father is working up to the present moment, and I am working." He didn't say "I am working as God the Son with the Father to sustain and govern the universe." He said, "I am working." The person, the God-man, was working. How the human nature participated in those particular works cannot be known, but in Scripture the deity nature always worked in harmony with the human nature, because the God-man was not God plus man, not God and man, but one person, the God-man. The universe did not fall apart when Jesus Christ died, it did not fall apart when his body lay dead in the grave: the God-man was living, conscious, active, and working.

Our discussion, our answer to the question, "Was Jesus the Christ living, conscious, and active between his physical death and the resurrection of his physical body?" will now turn to the incarnation. The purpose will be to demonstrate from Scripture Jesus Christ is the person God the Son in union with the genuine human body and genuine rational human soul of Jesus of Nazareth, thereby forming one person with one personality as informed by both deity and human natures. We should already see the end of our journey: a person never ceases his or her personal existence, whether in the body or out of the body. So too Jesus the Christ, the God-man.

Incarnation Of God With Man

The Bible presents God the Son's incarnation as a supra-naturally caused, non-sexual act of procreation, through a woman who was a virgin. I have previously discussed how the human soul may be formed through procreation. Just as the two gametes possess the parts from the parents necessary to form a new body, even so the two gametes possess the parts from the parents necessary to form a new soul.

The conception of Jesus Christ was not a normal procreation. There was only one gamete, Mary's ovum. Because Mary birthed a normal, genuine human being, we must assume by faith the Holy Spirit in some manner created *ex nihilo*, or perhaps formed from existing materials, all that was necessary to form a new male body and new male soul from Mary. The God who made the DNA that forms the body, and created the immaterial components (life, essence, attributes) that form the soul, had no problem supplying the necessary complements to

Mary's DNA and Mary's soul in order to form a male human being from one female gamete. (The conception was neither parthenogenesis nor androgenesis).

Did not God do something similar with Eve? God formed a female human being using Adam's DNA and Adam's soul. The simplest way to imagine (to form a mental image as an aid to understanding) what happened in Jesus' conception is to imagine the Holy Spirit created or formed a male gamete to join with Mary's gamete. But that is imagination, we don't know how the Holy Spirit caused Mary to conceive a normal genuine male human being using her female DNA and her female soul.

In every respect, the male human being conceived in Mary's body was a normal male human being (without the sin attribute that Mary carried in her human nature). That was why God the Son could form a union with this human body and human soul. God created humankind in his likeness and image. When God created Adam, i.e., the immaterial substantive entity (the soul) that was Adam, he was (so-to-speak) looking ahead to the incarnation. God the Son joined with a being whose human nature, in every aspect, was agreeable to his deity nature, because God Father-Son-Spirit had designed that human nature using God's own nature as the archetype. If, as seems reasonable, God used his own person as the archetype, then the essence and attributes of the human soul should reflect the archetype. (Genesis 5:1, 3 illustrate the point.) **Humankind created in God's image, Genesis 1:26–27, is a soul, a person, fashioned according to God's communicable attributes in finite measure, in a greater or lesser degree, depending on the attribute in question. Repeating from above:**

> Moral image: holiness, sanctification, righteousness, justice, mercy, faithfulness.
>
> Intellectual image: personality, will, volition, veracity, knowledge, wisdom.
>
> Spiritual image: love, compassion, goodness, kindness, longsuffering, mercy. [Quiggle, *God Became*, 42.]

Not one component of the image of God in humankind is physical. To use an illustration—it is only an illustration—God the Son joined in union with Jesus the human being as easily as hand-in-glove. It is an apt illustration because a glove is specifically made to fit the hand; it is apt because in the union of hand-in-glove neither the hand nor the glove merge or otherwise lose their particular attributes. The hand remains a hand, the glove remains a glove. The illustration is naturally limited because unlike a hand in a glove, the incarnation was a permanent union, with a genuine human person, initiated and maintained by God the Son.

I have previously mentioned the human soul of Jesus the human being did not have a personality when conceived. No human soul has a personality when conceived. A human soul is the indissoluble union of life, essence, and attributes. The individual human personality develops over time from the synergistic action of attributes, will, and life-experiences. Left on its own in the womb, the zygote and fetus will begin to develop a personality as it develops physically.

The zygote that was the newly conceived Jesus was not left on its own. God the Son immediately supplied his personality by incarnation at the moment conception occurred. The human nature of Jesus did not have a personality at the moment of conception, but it was a human nature: a complex of human attributes, part of the human soul. God the Son joined in union with that normal human soul, a human soul made by the Holy Spirit as sinless as the original (Adam) was when created, composed of life, essence, and attributes, but without personality, which the God the Son immediately supplied in the incarnation, thereby forming the deity-human person Jesus the Christ. As the human nature naturally developed in and out of the womb, it naturally developed a personality (Luke 2:52). The consciousness of the God-man was the blending of both natures, but it was the consciousness of one personality, that of God the Son, informed by both natures, and therefore never ceased to exist and never ceased to be living and active at any time between physical death and resurrection.

A Permanent Incarnation

The incarnate person Jesus Christ lived in body and soul. The incarnate person Jesus Christ physically died. The incarnate person Jesus Christ physically resurrected. The incarnate person Jesus Christ physically ascended. The incarnate person Jesus Christ sits at the right hand of God in heaven. The incarnate person Jesus Christ makes intercession for the believer. The incarnate person Jesus Christ is the believer's Advocate. The Scripture always speaks of the incarnate person as one person, not as two natures.

The incarnate person is the union of deity and humanity: God the Son in active and continuing union with the human soul Jesus. The incarnate person suffered the physical death of his body; the incarnate person reunited with his physical body in resurrection. Why then, would anyone propose, as Physicalist-Conditionalist proposes, that the union of God with man—the incarnate person—ceased to exist for the three days between the incarnate person's physical death and the bodily resurrection of the incarnate person? Why would anyone propose that in the union of God with man, as the Substance Dualist-Conditionalist proposes, that the man was unconscious-sleeping between the incarnate person's physical death and the bodily resurrection of the incarnate person? The incarnate person was not just man and not just deity, but deity and humanity in an indissoluble union.

Does Scripture say the incarnate person was living, conscious, and active during the three days of physical death? I previously proved it does. To the saved thief on the cross, Jesus said, "I say to you, today you will be in Paradise with me" (Luke 23:43). Regardless of what one believes "paradise" to be, Jesus said, "*Today* you will be in paradise with *me*." The "today" was the day of the death of the body. The "me" Jesus speaks of is himself, the incarnate person: not the deity, not the human, but the one person, the God-man, in continuing, active, conscious existence during the time he was separated from his body.

The saved thief, who would also die that day, would himself be in heaven with Jesus Christ, a living, conscious, active immortal disembodied soul. And the disbelieving, not-saved thief? In hades with all the other not-saved living, conscious, active immortal disembodied souls.

The person Jesus Christ expected to be in heaven (my view of paradise, 2 Corinthians 12:2, 4) immediately after his physical death. It is, perhaps, necessary to answer the objection that Jesus Christ did not go to heaven immediately after physical death, based on John 20:17, "**Jesus says to her, "Do not handle me, for I have not yet ascended to the Father; but go to my brothers and say to them, 'I am ascending to my Father and your Father, and to my God and your God.'"**

That objection is based on the failure to distinguish between his ascension ("I have not yet ascended") forty days later, and his presence in heaven immediately following his physical death, Luke 23:43. Jesus Christ was a believer in God, a worshiper of God, a person in a faith-based relationship with God. We tend not to think of him in those terms, but he was genuinely human. God designed human beings to believe in God, to worship God, to pray to God, to be in a faith-based relationship with God. Jesus did all those things because he was a genuine human being.

Therefore the principle Paul states at 2 Corinthians 5:8 must also apply to the incarnate person Jesus Christ. The biblical principle is, "absent from the body, present with the Lord." What applies to every human being who is in a faith-based relationship with God must apply to the God-man, who was and is as genuinely human as he was/is genuinely deity. Jesus Christ was in a faith-based relationship with God. As a human being, his human soul was immediately present with his Lord, the Triune God, immediately after his physical death, Luke 23:46. Then, three days later, the incarnate person reunited with his physical body.

Jesus the Christ as literally present with his Lord in heaven between physical death and resurrection is not in contradiction with the deity nature, which before the incarnation was omnipresent and continued to be omnipresent during and after the incarnation. As explained in the previous section, Jesus Christ had and continues to have a dual presence in the universe. From the moment of the incarnation there has continuously existed the unlimited, infinite omnipresence of the deity, and the limited-in-time-and-space finite presence of the humanity. Whether in the body of out of the body, the human soul of Jesus Christ always was and ever will be limited to one place at any one moment in time.

Therefore, at his physical death, the person Jesus Christ, the immaterial soul, was literally in heaven in the immediate presence of the Father, Luke 23:46, and he was at the same time literally omnipresent throughout the universe. In heaven, as deity he was omnipresent, but his disembodied finite human soul (the soul is the person) was strictly defined by time and space: in one place at any one time. When he returned to his body, he was both defined in time and space by that body and he was omnipresent throughout the universe. The incarnation was and is and always will be permanent under any and every circumstance.

Summary

The purpose of this chapter was to demonstrate from the Scripture that the person Jesus the Christ, the God-man, the Son of God was living, active, and conscious between physical death and physical resurrection. I have accomplished that purpose.

God the Son is an increate being who has life-in-himself.

The immaterial substantive entities known as human beings, once brought into existence through the processes of human procreation, are unconditionally immortal souls, because the spirit essence life is an integral, indissoluble part of their being, Genesis 2:7. The deity-human person Jesus Christ was living, active, and conscious between physical death and resurrection.

The human being Jesus of Nazareth is a created being: an immortal immaterial substantive entity (a "soul") in union with a material body. There is no known dissolution ("death") for a human soul, because human souls have the spirit essence life as an integral, indissoluble part of their being. The physical death of the body is when the person leaves the body. The person continues living, active, and conscious after the body dies (e.g., Matthew 17:1–3; Luke 16:23; 23:43, 46). Even so, the person Jesus was living, active, and conscious during the time his body was dead.

God the Son joined with the newly conceived human body and human soul of Jesus, an act known as the incarnation. Because the human soul Jesus was newly conceived, it did not have a personality. God the Son supplied the personality when he joined in union with the newly conceived human soul Jesus. Therefore it is proper to speak of the God-man as one person with two natures and one personality, the personality of God the Son, as informed by the union of the two natures. God the Son is always living, conscious, and active, therefore the God-man was living, conscious, and active during his physical death.

The incarnation was the permanent union of the eternal, increate God the Son with the immortal immaterial substantive entity Jesus. The union is permanent, forming one person, the deity-human person Jesus, who could not cease to exist during the physical death of the God-man's body, because God the Son did not cease to exist, and the human soul, once existing, is immortal.

The deity-human person formed by the incarnation has continuing conscious existence, because both the deity consciousness and the human consciousness have continuous conscious existence. The deity-human person Jesus Christ was living, active, and conscious between physical death and resurrection.

Contrary to Physicalism, God the Son did not become human in the incarnation, nor did he add humanity to his deity. God the Son joined in union with a human person. In the incarnation the deity remained fully deity, the humanity remained fully human, the two natures distinct but indivisible and inseparable, the properties of each nature "being preserved, and concurring in one Person and one Subsistence" [Shedd, *Dogmatic*, 2:62]. Therefore the physical death of the God-man could not and did not affect the deity nature of God the Son.

Contrary to Physicalist-Conditionalism, a human being is not merely a biological process, but is an independent immortal immaterial substantive entity placed in union with a material body. The immaterial substantive entity Adam was created independent of the body, created in the image and likeness of the immaterial God, and animated the body when placed by God in the body. Adam reproduced himself in his descendants: independent immortal immaterial substantive entities that are able to exist in union with their material body or separated from their material body. Therefore, the physical death of the God-man could not and did not affect the immaterial human part of the incarnate person.

Scripture always presents the deity-human Jesus Christ as a person: as one person with one personality, that of God the Son, informed by the two natures. Contrary to the Substance Dualist-Conditionalist, when the body of the God-man died, the incarnate person continued in living, active, consciousness between physical death and physical resurrection. God the Son is never in an unconscious or "sleeping" state. God the Son is the sentient personality of the incarnate person Jesus Christ. The deity consciousness, which never sleeps (Psalm 121:2–4), and the human consciousness, which is always active (e.g., 1 Samuel 28:11–19; Matthew 17:3), were the consciousness of Jesus Christ, the two in union together to form the living, active, consciousness of the God-man.

In summary, the Conditionalist, whether an Anthropological Physicalist-Materialist, a Substance Dualist, or a

Traditional Dualist, has an incomplete understanding of the incarnation. The Conditionalist's doctrine, that the human part of Jesus Christ either ceased to exist, or lost consciousness, during the time his material body was dead, assumes God the Son incarnated with a human personality. No. God the Son incarnated with a human nature, material and immaterial, thereby becoming one person with two natures and one personality. The one person, God the Son incarnate in Jesus of Nazareth (thereby becoming Jesus the Christ), is always living, conscious, active.

Was the person Jesus the Christ living, active, and conscious between his physical death and physical resurrection? Yes. And if the immortal immaterial substantive human being Jesus of Nazareth was living, active, and conscious between his physical death and physical resurrection, so also all immortal immaterial substantive human beings; all of us, from Adam to the end of the universe. The physically dead persons Samuel and Moses appearing after physical death, the saved thief promised living, conscious, active existence after physical death, and the Rich Man, Lazarus, and Abraham seen after death example the intrinsic immortality of all human souls.

The Endless Conscious Suffering of the Unsaved

An Exegesis of Matthew 25:46

Introduction

The Conditionalist states the "Traditionalists" (2,000 years of historic orthodox Christianity) use Matthew 25:46 as the source for the doctrine of endless conscious punishment.

> It is this reference to "eternal punishment" that is seen as a slam dunk, proving beyond a reasonable doubt that hell is a place of eternal conscious suffering. [https://rethinkinghell.com/2014/01/15/matthew-2546-does-not-prove-eternal-torment-part-1/]

Of course, that is hyperbole, as that Annihilationist-Conditionalist writer knows—he goes on to discuss other scriptures. The biblical doctrine of the endless conscious suffering of the unsaved is supported by many scriptures. It is simply easier to build a straw-man argument by isolating one from all others.

The purpose of this chapter is to discuss and disprove the-Conditionalist's annihilationist argument (all varieties of Evangelical Conditionalists are annihilationist). That will be done through an exegesis Matthew 25:46, and by a little common sense reasoning, by comparing Matthew 25:46 and its key words with other scriptures, and by demonstrating Matthew 25:46 does teach the endless conscious suffering of the unsaved.

(Notice to the reader. In this chapter I use words and concepts that I have defined and explained in the first chapter.

For example, life, death, eternal life, immortality, the soul, etc. I will briefly define such words and concepts in this chapter, but please see the first chapter for a complete discussion.)

The Conditionalist Argument for Annihilationism

How does Matthew 25:46 read? "And these will go away into eternal punishment, but the righteous into eternal life."

Scripture defines eternal punishment as the duration of the punishment. The Conditionalist redefines eternal punishment as the duration of the consequences of punishment. In Conditionalism the consequence of endless punishment is endless non-existence. The following is the Conditionalist's view.

> It should come as no surprise, then, that in Matthew 25:46, when Jesus speaks of two mutually exclusive final destinies, one of them is "eternal life." The alternative, "eternal punishment," must therefore be the everlasting punishment of death forever, not embodied immortality and eternal life in hell, as the doctrine of eternal torment teaches. Of course, the punishment of execution doesn't consist in the process of dying, for if it were, a death-row criminal who gasps back to life, moments after being killed on the electric chair, would be released. No, the punishment of execution consists in the result of dying, namely, the ongoing privation of embodied life.
>
> As Augustine puts it, "as to the award of death for any great crime ... the laws reckon the punishment to consist ... in this, that the offender is eternally banished from the society of the living" [Schaff, *NPNF*, First

Series, vol. 2, *City of God*, 21.11.].

The eternal punishment of the wicked, therefore, inflicted by eternal fire, is the punishment of death forever—just as we Conditionalists contend. [https://rethinkinghell.com/2020/07/06/falling-into-error-grasping-at-straws-in-matthew-2546/]

Now this is as foolish and reductionistic as saying when a criminal is sentenced to prison, the duration of imprisonment is the punishment. No, being imprisoned is the punishment. The duration of imprisonment is one part of that punishment. If the sentence is execution is it the soul that is killed, or the body? Therefore, if the sentence is execution, it is the body is killed, and it is the body that is endlessly dead, not the soul.

Do souls continue after physical death? I have shown abundantly in chapter one the disembodied soul continues living, conscious, and active after physical death. To that argument one might add the disembodied souls of Revelation 6:9; 7:9; 14:9–11 (what is in view in 14:9–11 is hades and Gehenna).

In the Conditionalist doctrine, the purpose of punishment in the lake of fire is to render the unsaved person non-existent. All Conditionalists say, "in Matthew 25:46, when Jesus speaks of two mutually exclusive final destinies, one of them is eternal life." According to the Conditionalist, the only alternative to eternal life is, "eternal punishment," which must be (quoting) "the punishment of death forever." By "the punishment of death forever" the Conditionalist means forever non-existent.

What is Eternal Life

To understand what the Conditionalist means by "death forever," one must understand what the Conditionalist means by "eternal life," compared to what the Scripture means by "eternal life." The Conditionalist defines eternal life as immortality of body (and soul for some Conditionalists), but defines the opposite of immortality as non-existence.

> When the gift of life is ultimately granted forever, we call that immortality. We also call it eternal life. [https://rethinkinghell.com/2019/07/20/conditional-immortality-meaning-best-label/]

In the Scripture, eternal life is not the same as immortality. In Scripture, "eternal life" is more than duration of life, e.g., John 17:3, eternal life is also a quality of life (see chapter 1 for a complete definition). At Romans 6:23, eternal life is contrasted with death both spiritual and physical, and therefore eternal life must be both spiritual life as a quality of life, and physical life. At John 3:15; 10:28, Jesus said everyone to whom he gave eternal life would never perish. But believers do perish: they die; to date every believer has died, or will die (unless raptured 1 Corinthians 15:51–52). Therefore, that "eternal life" Jesus gives the believer, must be something more than endless duration of physical life.

The issue is not trivial, or a dispute over words. The Conditionalist defines salvation as immortality given *after* resurrection. (Hence "conditional" immortality: some receive it, some don't.) Conditionalists believe immortality is, "a gift bestowed by God upon his children" [https://rethinkinghell.com/explore/] after physical death and resurrection. As noted above, receipt of immortality is salvation in Conditionalism; or using their own words, receipt of immortality "determines who is a child of God" [https://rethinkinghell.com/explore/].

The reader will have noticed the words "after physical death and resurrection" are not part of the quote from that particular article on the "Rethinking Hell" website. The reason is the site is a maze of articles that never quite touch on the subject of when immortality is granted, tending to focus on the annihilation of the unsaved. But that it is their doctrine is clear from the following statements.

> God alone possesses immortality innately and therefore any other being who is immortal (imperishable, deathless) is so extrinsically, that is, as the result of a positive act of God. [https://rethinkinghell.com/explore/]

No, God is eternal, not immortal. To be eternal is to be without beginning and without end, to be immortal is to have a beginning but no end. God created the human soul as immortal, and gives immortality to the body after resurrection.

> Conditionalism is the view that life is the Creator's provisional gift to all, which will ultimately be granted forever to the saved and revoked forever from the unsaved. When the gift of life is ultimately granted forever, we call that immortality. We also call it eternal life. Salvation, on our view, is salvation to everlasting life with God. Simultaneously, it is salvation from a permanent death (termination of life forever; final loss of being).

[https://rethinkinghell.com/2019/07/20/conditional-immortality-meaning-best-label/]

In Evangelical Conditionalism, salvation is after resurrection, when God gives immorality to soul and body.

> In denying that all seek and receive the gift of eternal life, which we associate with immortality, we are denying universal immortality. We are denying that all people ever to have lived will live forever.
> [https://rethinkinghell.com/2019/07/20/conditional-immortality-meaning-best-label/]

In biblical, historical, orthodox Christianity, eternal life is a quality of life, as well as a duration of life. Salvation, and therefore eternal life, is prior to physical death, not conditional after resurrection.

> Conditionalism is the view that life is the Creator's provisional gift to all, which will ultimately be granted forever to the saved and revoked forever from the unsaved.
> [https://rethinkinghell.com/2019/07/20/conditional-immortality-meaning-best-label/]

Reader, understanding the difference between immortality and eternal life is critical to orthodox Christianity. Scripturally, eternal life is salvation, immortality is not salvation. Evangelical Conditionalism is wholly outside the orthodoxy of biblical, historical Christianity.

Eternal life is a quality of life God gives the believing sinner during this present mortal life that changes the believer from sinner to saved and regenerates their human nature to born-again. The eternal life of the saved is a quality of life God imparts or adds to the believer at salvation, wherein he shares his communicable attributes in a measure suitable to a finite being, changing them into the image of Christ during this mortal life, Romans 8:29. Eternal life is the "seed" that grows into a life of habitual righteousness in the believer, 1 John 3:9. The believer's eternal life is endless once received. The eternal life given the believer endures throughout mortal life, is not overcome by physical death (the believer's immortal soul is in heaven, 2 Corinthians 5:8), and continues endlessly in the immortal life of body and soul the believer experiences after resurrection in the presence of God, Revelation 3:12, without end.

What about Conditionalism? What the Conditionalist means by "eternal life" is immortality. Immortality of the physical body for the Conditionalist Physicalist; immortality of body and soul for other varieties of Conditionalists. Evangelical Conditionalism's plan of salvation is this: After resurrection, some people are given by God the gift of immortality and others are not. Those who are not given the gift of immortality are annihilated—made non-existent—in the lake of fire.

The above was laboriously put together from various articles on the "Rethinking Hell" website. In Conditionalism, either you are saved after resurrection by being given immortality, or you are annihilated after resurrection because you were not given immortality.

The basis for the reward of immortality is defined in Evangelical Conditionalism as God elected some to receive immortality after resurrection. That is not biblical salvation.

The Conditionalist doctrine immediately raises the question, if God has chosen to give some believers immortality after resurrection, then what is their fault that those believers do not receive immortality during this mortal life? Is the basis of immortality faith? And if faith, then why does not faith receive immortality during this mortal life when faith is being exercised? Immediately the informed Christian suspects the Conditionalist's salvation (immortality) is a reward for works demonstrating faithfulness. However, the Evangelical Conditionalist does not say, because he does not know. There is no assurance of salvation in Evangelical Conditionalism, unlike biblical salvation, 1 John 5:11–13.

What about the unsaved—the ones not receiving immortal life after resurrection? One cannot rationally or logically compare or contrast the Scripture doctrine of endless eternal life with the Conditionalist doctrine of endless non-existence. As Charles Ryrie said, "Logic and implications do have their appropriate place. God's revelation is orderly and rational, so logic has a proper place in the scientific investigation of that revelation. When words are put together in sentences, those sentences take on implications that the theologian must try to understand" [Ryrie, *Basic*, 18].

There is a rule of logic that states to have a basis for comparison (or contrast) one must make sure the two things have enough in common.

Applying the rule of comparison, and basing these comparisons on the teaching of Scripture as a whole, what do saved and unsaved persons have in common, and in what do they contrast?

    In common, according to the Scripture.

        Saved and unsaved are human beings

        Saved and unsaved are alive in body and soul

        Saved and unsaved are an immaterial immortal soul in a material mortal body

        Saved and unsaved will experience physical death

        Saved and unsaved will continue after physical death as a disembodied immortal soul

        Saved and unsaved will be resurrected in body and the soul reunited with the body

        Saved and unsaved will continue living endlessly as immortal soul in immortal body after their respective resurrections

    In contrast, according to the Scripture.

        The saved resurrected body and soul are endlessly immortal and incorruptible.

        The unsaved resurrected body and soul are endlessly immortal and corruptible.

        The saved live endlessly in the presence of God.

        The unsaved live endlessly in the lake of fire.

    The Conditionalist's comparison using Matthew 25:46, of the eternal life of the saved versus the eternal non-existence of the unsaved, is incorrect because it both misrepresents Scripture and fails the test of logic. Endless non-existence is not the logical opposite of endless life. The logical opposite of endless life is endless death. And as the Scripture defines endless life—eternal life—as both the quality and duration of life, then endless death must be both the quality and duration of life. And as Scripture defines death as separation, then endless death must mean some kind of endless separation. The Scripture defines that endless separation as the "second death," which is endless separation from the immediate and effective presence of God in the lake of fire. Let us discuss these things.

In the Scripture, eternal life is not simply immortality, but is predominantly a quality of endless life. Therefore the rational comparison is between the quality of life lived by the saved versus the quality of life lived by the unsaved, after physical death has occurred. Scripture presents life after death as endless for both saved and unsaved, therefore the correct comparison in Matthew 25:46 is in the quality of endless life lived by saved versus the quality of endless life lived by unsaved. As I will show, the Scripture teaches:

> The saved will experience endless eternal life in God's effective presence (God's effective presence is not his omnipresence but God at work in a person's life).
>
> The unsaved will experience endless life in the spiritual state known as the second death, separated from God's effective presence, subject to his just wrath.

Therefore, applying the rule of comparison and contrast, contrary to the Conditionalist, the point of comparison is the quality of that endless life both saved and unsaved will experience. Not endless non-existence as the consequence of punishment, contra Conditionalism, but the punishment itself, which is endlessly suffering the wrath of God in the lake of fire, which was designed to accomplish that very purpose, for it is an unquenchable fire.

Even the Conditionalist says the unsaved must suffer punishment in the lake of fire; but like so many other cults, they give that endless punishment an unbiblical ending.

If, as is the case, the result of the eternal life of the saved is the quality of life: present in the effective presence of God in endless conscious bliss; then the result of the punishment of the unsaved must also be the quality of life: separated from the effective presence of God in endless conscious suffering.

Death and the Second Death

The Conditionalist defines endless punishment as causing a kind of death that results in non-existence, therefore endless "death." Their doctrine confuses death with non-existence.

What is death? When interpreting Scripture, it is always helpful to use Scripture's terms and understand those terms as Scripture defines them. The Bible names the Conditionalist "punishment of death forever" as the "second death," Revelation 2:11; 20:6, 14; 21:8 (all uses). The punishment of the unsaved is not non-existence forever, but the second death forever.

One of the significant issues troubling Conditionalist doctrine is the unwillingness, or perhaps the inability, to understand and use Scripture terms as Scripture defines those terms. Instead, the Conditionalist redefines biblical terms to suit their doctrine. In the bit of Conditionalist illogic quoted in the introduction to this chapter, the Scripture term misused by the Conditionalist is "death." In Scripture, death never means non-existence.

In the Scripture, death is separation, not non-existence. The Physicalist-Conditionalist (no soul, life is material only) believes both the first death (physical death) and the second death (Revelation 20:14) are physical deaths resulting (both times) in non-existence. All other kinds of Conditionalists (known as "Substance Dualist" and "Traditional Dualist") believe only the second death results in non-existence.

The Physicalist-Conditionalist tries to avoid the issue of non-existence in the first death by saying the person in the grave is dead, not non-existent. The Physicalist-Conditionalist gets away with that by using the same means the stage magician uses to fool his audience: by focusing their attention elsewhere, i.e., on the body rather than the non-existent soul of Physicalism. In Physicalism-Conditionalism, when the body dies, the person "produced" as an effect of biological processes ceases to exist.

The Physicalist-Conditionalist defines life in strictly physical terms: a physical body only, not an immaterial soul also. So he focuses attention on the physical condition of the body in death, which obviously lies in the grave, and therefore is not non-existent. But let us remember the Physicalist defines the person as the mind, and in Physicalism the mind is an observable side effect of physical biological processes. Applying a bit of rational logic to the Physicalist's doctrine, when the biological processes cease to function in physical death, the mind, i.e., the person, must cease to exist, for the person's existence depends on the biological processes. Therefore, in Physicalism-Conditionalism, the person becomes non-existent as a result physical death.

What saith the Word of God? According to Scripture, physical death is when the soul separates from the body. The first human body was inert, non-living matter until joined with the soul, Genesis 2:7, indicating the animating principle "life" is within the soul. Should the soul leave the body, the body must return to inert, non-living matter, Genesis 3:19, because the animating principle "life" is part of the soul, and the soul has left the body.

The universal experience of humankind from Adam to the present and into the yet-future verifies the body is lifeless without the animating soul. Indeed, the worldly definition of death is the absence of life, so determined because the "signs of life" are absent. The worldling cannot empirically prove the existence of a soul, and therefore denies its existence (hence Physicalism), and therefore cannot understand death is when the person leaves the body.

In Scripture, at physical death, the body becomes inert and decomposes, the soul continues in life active and conscious in the spirit domain. The soul was created apart from the body, independent of the body, living when not joined with the body, animating the body when joined with the body; Genesis 2:7. The person, the immaterial soul, is in union with the material body, not a unity with the body. When the body dies the person, the soul, continues in life.

We know this is true because Scripture has given us the

example of two people who physically died and then were physically seen after their physical death as conscious and active disembodied souls. I am referring to the prophet Samuel, 1 Samuel 28:11–19, and Moses the Law-giver, Matthew 17:1–3. These are clearly instances of a living, conscious, active person between physical death and resurrection. A third instance is the rich man, Luke 16:23, and the beggar Lazarus, 16:24, and Abraham (same reference). (Even if this narrative is a parable, it still describes the consequences of physical death [Quiggle, *Dispensational*, 138–143]. A parable, unlike a fable, is built with literal elements.) The thief saved on the cross is another example, for he was promised living, active, consciousness in heaven after his physical death.

The other kind of death in the Scripture is spiritual death, which is the person (the soul) separated from the effective presence of God: in a word, unsaved. All persons are in the state of spiritual death until saved, but some remain spiritually dead without hope of salvation when their unsaved condition continues through their physical death. Physical death seals the unsaved person in their unsaved, spiritually dead state. That is the power of physical death: "it awaits for men to die once, that after that judgment" (Hebrews 9:27).

Returning to the discussion of the "second death." In the context of the Revelation 20 passage, the first death is the unsaved sinner's physical death, which confirms the unsaved sinner in his or her spiritual state of unsaved, spiritually dead, spiritually separated from God. The second death is the endless separation of the unsaved sinner from God's effective presence through his or her endless residence in the lake of fire, there to endure God's just wrath in endless conscious suffering. The lake of fire was designed by God to enact God's just wrath against the unsaved sinner, Matthew 25:41 (the Conditionalist agrees with the punishment, but says the ultimate purpose of punishment is to annihilate the sinner's existence body and soul.)

The Conditionalist says, "The eternal punishment of the wicked … is the punishment of death forever." No, if you define "death forever" as non-existence. Yes, if you define "death forever" scripturally. In the terms used and defined by Scripture, "the eternal punishment of the unsaved is the endless punishment of the second death forever." The second death means confirmed in spiritual death forever: spiritually and physically separated from God in endless conscious suffering under God's wrath, which is executed according to God's justice against the unsaved sinner's confirmed and continuous rebellion against God; continuous because there is no salvation or annihilation in the lake of fire, Revelation 20:14–15.

In Scripture, death is always separation: the soul is separated from the body: physical death; the soul is separated from God: spiritual death. The second death (Revelation 20:46) is the consequence of the endless spiritual death of the person dying with their sins unforgiven, therefore unsaved. That consequence is even as Revelation 20:14 says it is, "And Death and hades were thrown into the lake of fire. This the second death is the lake of fire." The second death is permanent, endless, conscious separation from God, endlessly suffering the wrath of God.

Augustine: Of Hell, and the Nature of Eternal Punishments

To support their view of endless punishment as the endless consequence of non-existence, we saw above that the Conditionalist turns to Augustine, in his work, *City of God*, book 21, chapter 11 (abbreviated as 21.11). As I will show, Augustine does not support the Conditionalist view that "death forever" means non-existence, because his quote is taken out of context by the Conditionalist: it does not mean what the Conditionalist says it means. I will repeat the Augustine quote as given by the Conditionalist.

> as to the award of death for any great crime ... the laws reckon the punishment to consist ... in this, that the offender is eternally banished from the society of the living. [Schaff, *NPNF*, *City of God*, 21.11.]

By "eternally banished from the society of the living," Augustine is not arguing for non-existence. The context of Augustine's argument is that the duration of punishment for a crime (not the consequence of the punishment, but the punishment itself) is not equal to the duration of time in which the crime was committed or practiced. For example (*City of God*, 21.11), a heinous crime that may have lasted for a great length of time (a modern example: a serial killer) is punished in a brief moment of time by execution. Augustine gives a crystal clear example.

> But if scourging [beaten with a whip or rod] be a reasonable penalty for kissing another man's wife, is not the fault of an instant visited with long hours of atonement, and the momentary delight punished with lasting pain? Schaff, *NPNF*, *City of God*, 21.11.]

Applying Augustine's argument to Conditionalist doctrine, the punishment for a mortal life of unforgiven sinning is not the endlessness of non-existence, but an existence of endless punishment; or as Augustine puts it, "lasting pain." Have I misunderstood Augustine?

If the Conditionalists really wanted to know what Augustine thought about eternal punishment, they would have turned back two sections in *City of God* from 21:11 to 21.9, the section titled, "Of Hell, and the Nature of Eternal Punishments." (But of course they pretend that section does not exist.) At the beginning of that section Augustine references Isaiah 66:24. That scripture divides into three sections.

> 66:24a, And they shall go forth and look on the corpses of the men who have transgressed against me,
>
> 66:24b, Because their worm does not die and their fire is not quenched,
>
> 66:24c, and they shall be an abhorrence to all flesh.

How did Jesus use this scripture—because Augustine draws his doctrine "Of Hell, and the Nature of Eternal Punishments" from Jesus.

One might suppose this is a reference to corpses, except Jesus used only 66:24b to describe the endless punishment in Gehenna, the place of unquenchable fire. Jesus' use of the Isaiah quote is *highlighted*, below.

> Mark 9:43–47, And if your hand might cause you to stumble, cut it off. It is better for you to enter into life maimed rather than, having two hands, to go away into

Gehenna—into the unquenchable fire *where their worm dies not, and the fire is not quenched*. And if your foot might cause you to stumble, cut it off. It is better for you to enter into life lame rather than, having two feet, to be cast into Gehenna—into the unquenchable fire *where their worm dies not, and the fire is not quenched*. And if your eye might cause you to stumble, cast it out. It is better for you with one eye to enter into the kingdom of God, than having two eyes to be cast into Gehenna. *where their worm dies not, and the fire is not quenched*.

How did Augustine interpret, "their worm dies not, and the fire is not quenched"?

> In that future punishment both body and soul shall be burned with fire, while the soul shall be, as it were, gnawed by a worm of anguish ... it is absurd to suppose that either body or soul will escape pain in the future punishment. [*City of God*, 21.9.]

Did Augustine view that "future punishment" as the non-existence of Conditionalism, or as endless conscious suffering? Though his science may be wrong (in the quote below) his doctrine is unmistakable.

> For I have already sufficiently made out that animals can live in the fire, in burning without being consumed, in pain without dying, by a miracle of the most omnipotent creator, to whom no one can deny that this is possible, if he be not ignorant by whom has been made all that is wonderful in all nature. [*City of God*,

21.9.]

Without question, Augustine did not view endless punishment as the endlessness of non-existence, but as endless conscious suffering. So too, all the early church, with the exception of a few apostates preaching the annihilation of body and soul. (Should one doubt God is able to make something burn without being consumed, see Exodus 3:2.)

Jesus and Augustine referencing Isaiah 66:24b reveals another distortion of Scripture by the Conditionalists. In one article the Conditionalist writer refers to Matthew 18:8–9, which reads.

> But if your hand or your foot causes you to sin, cut them off and cast them from you. It is better for you to enter into life crippled or lame, than having two hands or two feet, to be cast into the eternal fire. And if your eye causes you to sin, take it out and cast it from you. It is better for you to enter into life one-eyed, than having two eyes to be cast into the fire of Gehenna.

In response the writer says.

> [Jesus] uses the phrase [the eternal fire] earlier, in Matthew 18:8–9, where it parallels τὴν γέενναν τοῦ πυρός, or, "the Gehenna of fire." Jesus's references to Gehenna, like this one, allude to such Old Testament passages as Jeremiah 7:32–33, in which Yahweh says, "it will no longer be called Topheth, or the Valley of the Son of Hinnom, but the Valley of Slaughter, for they will bury in Topheth, because there is no room elsewhere. And the dead bodies of this people will be food for the

birds of the air, and for the beasts of the earth, and none will frighten them away." Thus, by "eternal fire," Jesus means the fiery, death-dealing wrath of God. [https://rethinkinghell.com/2020/07/06/falling-into-error-grasping-at-straws-in-matthew-2546/]

The problems for this Conditionalist interpretation are insurmountable. One, Tophet (Topheth) is a place, not a person or an attribute. Two, the punishment in Tophet is endless: the bodies are endlessly physically dead. Three, the quality of an "eternal fire": if the word "eternal is to have any normal meaning, it is that the fire is unquenchable, it is endless. Four, Jesus never makes reference to "the Valley of the Son of Hinnom." Five, this is not Jesus only reference to Tophet. Six, Jesus' reference to Tophet is more likely Isaiah 30:33.

Looking at the last first, what does Isaiah 30:33 say? "For yes, from before Tophet was established, for the king it is prepared; he has made it deep and large, its pyre is fire with much wood, the breath of YHWH, like a stream of brimstone."

> In Isaiah 30:33 the place-name "Tophet" appears to be a designation for the lake of fire, because 1) it was established of old (cf. Matthew 25:41) and 2) Isaiah 30:33, "the breath of YHWH, like a stream of brimstone," kindles it.
>
> Revelation 19:20 describes the lake of fire as "burning with brimstone." Fire and brimstone is the portion of the wicked, Psalm 11:6, "He will rain coals upon the wicked, fire and brimstone and a burning wind will be the portion of their cup." [see Quiggle, *Mark*, 274.]

Tophet is the lake of fire. Jesus' reference to "the Gehenna of fire" in Matthew 18:9, is not to Tophet as the Valley of the Son of Hinnom, but to Tophet as the lake of fire, a place of everlasting fire.

Presuppositions in interpretation, such as the presupposition of annihilationism, distort the plain and normal meaning of the Scripture. If we look at every scripture where Jesus references Tophet, we discover Isaiah 66:24b (which I quoted above) used in Mark 9:43–48 (quoted above). When we consider all the places where Jesus makes reference to the Old Testament Tophet, it is clear Jesus thought of Tophet as the place of endless conscious suffering. Jesus did not use the first part of Isaiah 66:24, "And they shall go forth and look on the corpses of the men who have transgressed against me," but only the middle part, and that in connection to Gehenna, which Jesus defined as "the unquenchable fire," in agreement with Isaiah 66:24b, "Because their worm does not die and their fire is not quenched."

The word "worm" is a clear reference to physical corruption. If, as Jesus said (and as the God-man he should know) the "worm" of corruption does not die, then the corruption of the body must be endless; if the fire of punishment "shall not be quenched," then that punishment for which the unquenchable fire was created must be endless. Is God's omnipotence so limited he cannot create a human body both endlessly corruptible and immortal? Is God's omnipotence so limited he cannot create a fire that is unquenchable—a lake of fire that will endlessly burn yet not annihilate? God's omnipotence is not limited.

Reason asks, why would God create an unquenchable fire

at the beginning of the universe (when Satan and his angels sinned, Matthew 25:41), for one use one time only—according to the Conditionalist—for the annihilation of fallen angels and sinful human beings at the end of this present universe? The Great White Throne judgment, that the Conditionalist agrees takes place, occurs after the present universe is destroyed, Revelation 20:11, 2 Peter 3:10. The lake of fire continues burning, Revelation 21:8, after a new heaven and earth are created, Revelation 21:1.

> Revelation 21:8, But to fearful, and to unbelieving, and to having become abhorrent, and to murderers, and to sexually immoral, and to sorcerers, and to idolators, and to all liars, their portion is in the lake burning with fire and sulfur, which is the second death.

Why does the place of punishment continue in the new heaven and earth if its purpose is fulfilled in the annihilation of evil angels and unsaved human beings at the end of this present heavens and earth? Since the time the fallen angels sinned the lake of fire has been burning in anticipation of being occupied, Matthew 25:41, 46. That much is clear from the Scripture.

After the lake of fire has been occupied, Revelation 19:20; 20:11–15; 21:8, and has annihilated fallen angels and unsaved human beings—according to the annihilationism of Conditionalism—shall an unquenchable fire continue to burn, but without purpose? Yes, it continues, because it is unquenchable, and yes, its purpose continues, because the punishment of the unsaved is endless in the unquenchable fire.

Revelation 14:11 says (of those receiving the mark of the

beast, 14:10), "And the smoke of their affliction goes up to the ages of the ages. And there is no rest day and night for those worshiping the beast, and its image, and if anyone receives the mark of its name." At least one group of sinners endures endless punishment without annihilation.

Why make an "unquenchable" fire for one use only. Conditionalism might say "unquenchable" refers to the consequences of its actions against the unsaved, But the Word of God says "unquenchable fire," as though the fire continues to burn continuously—everlastingly—which is what Matthew 25:41 says it keeps on doing.

So there is it, an unquenchable fire in the Conditionalist's new heaven and earth, burning uselessly, unquenchably, everlastingly after fulfilling its purpose to annihilate fallen angels and human beings body and soul, making all non-existent. Why keep an unquenchable lake of fire burning everlastingly in a new universe if it has fulfilled its purpose? The more we compare Conditionalism with Scripture, the more absurd the doctrine is seen to be.

Reason also asks, why are unsaved sinners resurrected only to be annihilated. Could not the omnipotent God by divine fiat cause the non-existence of sinners at the moment of their physical death as the judgment for their unforgiven rebellion? (That is the doctrine of the Physicalist Conditionalist.) Why a resurrection of the non-existent for a little punishment and then again non-existence?

Or to ask the question in a different way, is not the purpose of an "unquenchable" fire, because the unsaved are resurrected to endless punishment? Therefore the purpose of the unquenchable fire must be as endless as the fire itself.

The Conditionalist is stuck with the unequivocable testimony of Scripture that sinners will be judged as to their just punishment, and then be cast into a lake of unquenchable fire as punishment justly adjudicated. So the Conditionalist must somehow conform that unquenchable fire to his doctrine. Conditionalism teaches both fallen angels and fallen human beings will be rendered non-existent by the everlasting, unquenchable fire. What does Scripture teach? The lake of fire is an unquenchable fire; an unquenchable fire implies the endless conscious suffering of fallen angels and sinful human beings, not their annihilation.

Our God is a perfectly rational God, and designed humankind to be rational. Which is more rational? Creating an everlasting, unquenchable fire that continues to burn without purpose after rendering human and angel sinners non-existent? Or endless conscious suffering in an everlasting, unquenchable fire to punish the criminal for his crimes committed against a holy God? We recognize some crimes are more serious, and thus deserve greater punishment, than other crimes. We fine a man who kills a dog; we execute a man who kills a fellow human being; how much more punishment is due the person who hates and rebels a lifetime, and beyond, against the thrice holy eternal God? The crimes of sin are a lifetime's work against a holy eternal God. The just punishment is endless conscious suffering, even as Jesus said, even as Augustine said.

Exegesis of Matthew 25:46

Matthew 25:46 reads "And these will go away into eternal punishment, but the righteous into eternal life."

The context of 25:46 is 25:31–45, a judgment of "nations" (25:32) when "the son of man comes in his glory" (25:31). How one interprets both the kingdom and judgment aspects of 25:31–45 passage is dependent on one's eschatology (Amillennial, Postmillennial, Premillennial), but the fact of judgment against the unbeliever at Christ's second coming is accepted by all biblically-based eschatologies. Even Evangelical Conditionalism accepts the fact of judgment.

In this judgment at Matthew 25:31–45, some persons will "inherit the kingdom prepared for you from the foundation of the world," 25:34. Again, one's eschatology determines the nature of that kingdom (Reformed: the eternal kingdom of Revelation 21–22; Dispensational: the Davidic-Messianic-Millennial kingdom of 2 Samuel 7:13, 16; Psalm 2; Revelation 20:1–7).

Contra Conditionalism, the contrast between those inheriting the kingdom (Matthew 25:34) and those not inheriting the kingdom (25:41) is not death but life: continuing life in the kingdom is contrasted with continuing life in the "eternal fire prepared for the devil and his angels." Death in the Bible is never annihilation but is separation: physical separation from life, spiritual separation from God.

When the context is considered, the contrast in 25:46, between "eternal life" and "eternal punishment," is not, as the Conditionalist states, between some kind of life and annihilation, but between the quality of life to be experienced by the inheritors (25:34) and the quality of life to be experienced by non-inheritors

(25:41). To say the quality of life experienced by non-inheritors is endless non-existence is an absurdity, for non-existence is no life at all.

Rationally, logically, there must be an equality between the two final destinies if the context and the judgment are to make a logical comparison. And so there is: life in the kingdom for the sheep; life in the everlasting fire for the goats. But the Conditionalist reads 25:33 and 25:41 much differently than what Jesus said. The Conditionalist reads like this:

> 25:33, "Come, those blessed of my Father, and inherit that eternal life prepared for you from the foundation of the world."
>
> 25:41, "Depart from me, you cursed, into the everlasting death [annihilation] prepared for the devil and his angels."

No. That is not what Jesus said, and that is not what Jesus meant. The passage compares one quality of life to another quality of life—life in the sense of where and how that life will be lived: life in the kingdom or life in the everlasting fire.

Looking to 25:46, the phrase "eternal punishment" describes "the eternal fire prepared for the devil and his angels," 25:41. We discover that eternal fire in a later passage.

> Revelation 20:10, And the Devil, the one deceiving them, was thrown into the lake of fire and sulfur, where also is the beast and false prophet. And they will be afflicted day and night to the ages of the ages.

The careful expositor notes two phrases in that passage.

The first is, the beast and false prophet of the Tribulation (Revelation 13) are already in that lake of fire, having been placed there—alive, not having passed through physical death—at Revelation 19:20. Whether one defines a thousand years (20:2, 3, 4, 5, 6, 7) as an indeterminate period of time (Reformed) or a literal time period of one thousand years (Dispensational), when Satan and the other fallen angels are cast into the lake of fire (where Satan goes, so go his fallen angels), the everlasting, unquenchable fire did not annihilate the beast and false prophet. They have been and are experiencing continuous conscious suffering. A thousand years have passed. When does this so-called annihilation into non-existence take place? The Conditionalist is more than willing to insert his annihilationist doctrine here, sensing an opportunity because Scripture does not say. The reason the Scripture does say is because the Scripture not teach annihilation.

The second phrase is "to the ages of the ages" (this is the literal rendering of the text, *aiṓn tón aiṓn*, that other versions render "forever and forever"). The devil and his angels will be "afflicted day and night to the ages of the ages" in the unquenchable fire of the lake of fire: from one age to the next, endlessly, forever and forever.

What is the age after this current age? Jesus tells us, "the kingdom prepared for you from the foundation of the world," Matthew 25:34. What is the age after the kingdom age? Jesus tells us, Revelation 21:1, "And I saw a new heaven and a new earth, for the first heaven and the first earth they had gone away." (Yes, at 21:1 the revelation of a new heaven and earth is from Jesus not John. Jesus gave the revelation to John, 1:1–2;

John is the scribe and publisher of the revelation.)

So the everlasting punishment of the lake of fire endures past the final age of this world, the kingdom, into the new age of a new heaven and a new earth, 21:8. And should there be another, unknown, age yet to come? The unquenchable fire continues to burn and continues to serve its purpose to the ages of the ages.

So also the unsaved human beings cast into the lake of fire, Matthew 25:41, 46, compare Revelation 20:14–15. The word *aiṓn* means "duration or continuance of time" [Zodhiates, s. v. 165]. Silva [*NIDNT*, 1:193], states *aiṓn* is used in the sense "eternity" by Plato, in the LXX, and in the New Testament. Silva says of *aiṓn* and the related *aiṓnios* (derived from *aiṓn*).

> The NT does not speak of an eternal death, possibly because the idea of eternity is so closely connected with life that the negation of eternal life can be understood only as the experience of ruin. Nevertheless, *aiṓnios* can be used to describe the future suffering of the ungodly: it modifies ... *púr* (fire) Matthew 18:8 ... 25:46."

When *aiṓn* is repeated, as it is here, the meaning is intensified: to all the ages; endlessly. The devil and his angels—and those human beings cast into the lake of fire with them—will suffer endlessly. Not endlessly non-existent, but endless conscious suffering. Matthew 25:41, 46; Revelation 20:10; 21:8 do not refer to punishment as endless non-existence. The Conditionalist teaches eternal punishment is not the punishment but the duration of the consequences of punishment, which (consequence) they define as non-existence. The Scripture teaches eternal punishment is exactly what the words say: endless conscious suffering.

An Examination of Key Words

I have from the Scripture proved Matthew 25:46 speaks of the endless conscious suffering of the unsaved. However, experience has taught me the skeptic, heretic, and apostate will always say, "But what about this? Doesn't this one thing cancel out all the scripture proofs you have given?" And so the Conditionalist:

> [W]hen other nouns of action are qualified as eternal [says the Conditionalist], it is often the results of the act, and not the act itself, that lasts for eternity. If this is even a reasonable possibility with Matthew 25:46, then we can no longer say that this proves the wicked always consciously exist; the one-time act of destroying them as punishment would yield the eternal result of them no longer being around ... annihilation is eternal punishment.
> [https://rethinkinghell.com/2014/01/15/matthew-2546-does-not-prove-eternal-torment-part-1/]

Therein lies the necessity to look at the three key words in Matthew 25:46. Those key words are "eternal, punishment, life." Respectively, the Greek words are: *aiōnios* (Strong's 166; G-K 173); *kólasis* (Strong's 2851; G-K 3136); *zōé* (Strong's 2222; G-K 2437).

Aiōnios (Strong's 166; G-K 173)

I examined *aiōnios* above. In Matthew 25:46 *aiōnios*

modifies *kólasis*, punishment. The concept of *aiōnios* is duration or continuance of time. The word is used seventy-one times in the New Testament. The majority of uses are associated with life. Does *aiōnios* in Matthew 25:46 refer to "the results of the act, and not the act itself" as the Conditionalist proposes? Let's find out.

The Greek *aiōnios* as used in the New Testament is among a group of words translated forever, everlasting, eternal, perpetual or age(s). As with any word in the Bible, this group of words is defined by each context in which they are used. A context where conditions change means the thing that is "forever, everlasting, eternal, perpetual," continues until the condition upon which those things were predicated changes. For example.

> Exodus 29:26–28, certain portions of meat from the offerings were to be for "Aaron and his sons by a statute forever." Here "forever" means "as long as the levitical priesthood and the sacrifices and offerings of the Mosaic Law are in effect."
>
> The mountains are "everlasting" and the hills are "perpetual," Habakkuk 3:6, until God scatters the mountains and bows the hills, same verse, compare Revelation 16:18, 20.
>
> The "everlasting" covenant of the rainbow endures until this present earth is replaced, because it was declared to be a sign this present earth would not ever again be destroyed with a flood, Genesis 9:11.

However, when the conditions do not change, the thing is

truly "forever, everlasting, eternal, perpetual." For example.

> YHWH is the "everlasting God," Genesis 21:33, meaning his existence is without beginning and without end.
>
> God made with David an "everlasting," covenant, 2 Samuel 23:5, a reference to the "forever" son and throne of 2 Samuel 7:12–13, 16, which is a reference to David's greater heir Christ. The Christ will begin his reign as King of kings and Lord of lords in his Davidic Kingdom commencing at his second advent, Revelation 20:4, continuing without end in the new heaven and earth, Revelation 21:1, 22–23.
>
> The person who savingly believes in Christ will have everlasting life, John 3:16. Because everlasting life comes from God, and God himself is everlasting, the everlasting life God gives his saved people is without end.

The lake of fire continues into a new heaven and earth. Therefore, the fire itself, as Jesus described it, is unquenchable, Mark 9:43, 45, 46, 48, and everlasting, Matthew 18:8; 25:41? Does Jesus or any Scripture give a rational reason to believe the unquenchable and everlasting fire has an end? If the fire is unquenchable and everlasting, is not the purpose of the fire unquenchable and everlasting?

I stress again that no Scripture teaches annihilation, without twisting the scriptures to fit the doctrine. If doctrine is developed from the teaching of the Scripture as a whole, and it should be, that doctrine is not the non-existence of annihilationism. Annihilationism, and its modern form

Conditionalism, is an aberration in the 2,000 years of historic orthodox Christianity. It is like Joseph Smith claiming God gave him previously unknown revelation to correct 1,830 years of error in the New Testament church. The claim stretches credulity beyond the boundaries of credibility. So also the annihilationism of Evangelical Conditionalism.

Other Scriptures make the point the fire is *aiōnios* in the sense of unquenchable and everlasting. For example, 2 Timothy 2:10, "Because of this, I endure all things for the sake of the elect, so that they also may obtain salvation in Christ Jesus, with eternal [*aiōnios*] glory." The glory itself is eternal, not some result of glory. Hebrews 5:9, "And having become fully qualified, he became to all those obeying him the source of eternal [*aiōnios*] salvation."

The salvation itself is eternal, not some result of salvation. It is the reality of an eternal (endless) salvation that requires an eternal (endless) punishment. But let us argue as the Conditionalist would argue. If, as is the case, the consequence of eternal life is endless conscious continuance in the presence of God, then isn't the consequence of eternal punishment endless conscious separation from the presence of God? Yes. Otherwise the logic is illogical, the comparison nonsensical.

The consistent use of *aiōnios* to indicate the idea of "endless" in relation to life, glory, and salvation, sixty-four times, indicates the same meaning should be considered in the other seven uses. These seven uses are.

> Matthew 18:8, But if your hand or your foot causes you to sin, cut them off and cast them from you. It is better

for you to enter into life crippled or lame, than having two hands or two feet, to be cast into the eternal [*aiṓnios*] fire.

Matthew 25:41, "And then he will say to those on the left, 'Depart from me, you cursed, into the eternal [*aiṓnios*] fire prepared for the devil and his angels.

Matthew 25:46, And these will go away into eternal [*aiṓnios*] punishment, but the righteous into eternal [*aiṓnios*] life.

Mark 3:29, But whoever should blaspheme against the Holy Spirit never has forgiveness forever [*aiṓn*], but is guilty of an eternal [*aiṓnios*] sin.

2 Thessalonians 1:9, These will suffer the penalty of eternal [*aiṓnios*] ruin away from the presence of the Lord and from the glory of his power.

Hebrews 6:2, teaching about baptisms, and of laying on of hands, of resurrection of the dead, and of eternal [*aiṓnios*] judgment.

Jude 7, as Sodom and Gomorrah, and the cities around them in the same manner with them, having practiced fornication and having followed after strange flesh, are set forth as an example to suffer the penalty of eternal [*aiṓnios*] fire.

There is no contextual reason why the meaning of *aiṓnios* in the above seven scriptures should be different from the meaning in the other sixty-four scriptures. One must import the doctrine of annihilationism into these seven scriptures in order to "discover" the doctrine in those scriptures.

Let's take a brief look at each.

Matthew 18:8. The Conditionalist says, "[Jesus] uses the phrase [the eternal fire] earlier, in Matthew 18:8–9, where it parallels τὴν γέενναν τοῦ πυρός, or, 'the Gehenna of fire.' Jesus's references to Gehenna, like this one, allude to such Old Testament passages as Jeremiah 7:32–33, in which Yahweh says, "it will no longer be called Topheth," etc. [https://rethinkinghell.com/2020/07/06/falling-into-error-grasping-at-straws-in-matthew-2546/].

The argument is Tophet, or Gehenna is a place on earth for dead bodies, and therefore not eternal.

I addressed this scripture above, and pointed out the five insurmountable problems with the Conditionalist's interpretation. Not the least is Jesus is referencing Isaiah 30:33; Psalm 11:6, not the Jeremiah passage, and those passages accurately describe the lake of fire.

The place known as "Gehenna," is the Greek word *géenna*. We know *géenna* is the lake of fire. Jesus speaks of a specific place that was composed of fire. The "*géenna* the [one] of fire [*púr*]," is a place made of fire. In Matthew 13:42, 50, it is a "furnace of fire." By definition "the *géenna* the [one] of *púr*" is the same as "the lake the [one] of *púr*," in Revelation 19:20; 20:10, 14, 15. Jesus describes it as "unquenchable fire" [Quiggle, *Life*, 89–95].

A fire that is "unquenchable" is *aiōnios*. The condition, unquenchable, never changes, so the fire is endless. An endless fire for an endless punishment. If the endless punishment is endless non-existence, then the fire serves no purpose after inflicting its punishment; yet the fire continues to burn, endlessly, from the ages to the ages.

Matthew 25:41, 46. I addressed the Conditionalist's misinterpretation of these verses in an earlier section.

Mark 3:29. This scripture is not speaking of the endless consequence of non-existence; it doesn't even mention endless punishment. The Conditionalist's distortion of this verse is a lesson on how not to interpret the Bible: "The person who commits the "eternal sin" is not doing the act for eternity" [https://rethinkinghell.com/2014/01/15/matthew-2546-does-not-prove-eternal-torment-part-1/], and therefore, says the Conditionalist, the punishment for this sin is not endless.

No serious Bible student would interpret the verse in that way. This scripture tells us the consequence of blasphemy against the Holy Spirit is no forgiveness forever, thus an "eternal" sin, i.e., the judicial guilt of "unforgiven" endures forever. Other scriptures tell us the consequence of unforgiven sin: endless punishment in the lake of fire.

2 Thessalonians 1:9. The Conditionalist article I read on this verse spent most of its energy talking about those interpreters and their interpretations that *do not* support Conditionalism. [https://rethinkinghell.com/2016/12/05/annihilation-in-2-thess-1-9-part-2-separation-or-obliteration/]. There is also a lot of argumentation about grammar and prepositions that obscure the main issue. I am going to skip to the writer's defense and

conclusions. Remember, these are the Conditionalist's comments.

> The presence of the Lord brings about destruction to the unholy; it literally kills and consumes those who have not had their sin covered.
>
> Eternal destruction, which is the consensus of all translations concerned with the Greek at all, conveys (this from Merriam-Webster Dictionary) the sense of 'the act or process of damaging something so badly that it no longer exists or cannot be repaired.
>
> The fact that the apostle Paul does not once mention everlasting torment is a bit of a scandal, and 2 Thessalonians 1:9 is the only passage that traditionalists are able to appeal to as describing any kind of eternal fate for sinners.
>
> We have yet another passage that explicitly describes final punishment in terms of affliction leading to destruction.

The word the Conditionalist so conveniently translates "destruction," and then uses a secular dictionary to define, is the Greek *ólethros* (briefly mentioned in the first chapter). This word means "ruin, destruction." As Zodhiates says [s. v. 3639], "The fundamental thought is not annihilation by any means, but unavoidable distress and torment." Silva agrees [*NIDNT*, s. v. 3897], *ólethros* means "eternal destruction understood as exclusion from the presence of the Lord." Only by abandoning the meaning of *ólethros* as it was used by the ancient Greeks and the biblical writers can the Conditionalist create his doctrine.

One of the unavoidable facts about the Conditionalist's defense of their doctrine is the tendency to select specific English translations of certain words that may be used in that defense; and to use secular dictionaries that provide little or no information of ancient secular and biblical use. Every word in any language has what is known as "semantic range," which is different meanings according to cultural use and context. For example, the simple English word "run" has over 100 meanings. A few examples: I ran a mile; I ran a business; I ran my car into the ground; I ran down his reputation.

Cultural use determines meaning. Moreover, word meanings change over time. That is why there are books about the ancient Greek language used in the Bible (Koine Greek), known as lexicons, to explain the vocabulary meaning, as well as books known as theological dictionaries or expository dictionaries that explain an ancient word's meaning according to use and context in the Scripture.

The Conditionalist is also very selective (dishonest?) in his use of modern words and dictionaries. For example, The Merriam-Webster Dictionary (online edition) defines "destruction" in this way: "the state or fact of being destroyed: RUIN." Why don't the Conditionalists base their doctrine on that definition?

If we translate 2 Thessalonians 1:9 according to the information supplied by secular Greek use, Zodhiates' *Expository Dictionary*, Silva's *NIDNT*, and Kittel's *Theological* Dictionary, as well as the *Merriam-Webster* dictionary used by the Conditionalist, then 2 Thessalonians 1:9 reads, "These will suffer the penalty of eternal ruin away from the presence of the Lord."

Not non-existence, but ruin in the sense of the quality of life.

The other thing sound interpretation notices is 2 Thessalonians 1:9 declares eternal *ólethros* for those "not obeying the gospel of our Lord Jesus," but does not at all describe the nature of that eternal *ólethros*. That job is left to other scriptures, such as Psalm 11:6; Isaiah 30:33; 66:24b; Mark 9:43–47; Revelation 20:11–15; 21:8. To discover the doctrine of non-existence in 2 Thessalonians 1:9, one must import the doctrine into that scripture; which is eisegesis not exegesis.

Of interest, is that one of the Conditionalist's favorite words, *apóllumi*, used in Matthew 10:28, is derived from *ólethros*, and with the same meaning, "ruin." I thoroughly discussed this word in the first chapter under the heading, "The Humanity of the God-man," subheading, "An Immortal Soul."

Scripture never states the dissolution (annihilation) of the soul. The complete absence in Scripture of the annihilation of the soul is the complete absence of support for the doctrines of annihilationism. Whether *ólethros* or *apóllumi*, the word in both Scripture and ancient secular use means "ruin" of some kind, never annihilation (regardless of how carefully selected English versions translate the words).

One final word on 2 Thessalonians 1:9. What does "away from the presence of the Lord" mean. We have already validated that "eternal punishment" refers to endless conscious suffering in the Lake of Fire. Part of that suffering is sometimes referred to as separated from God, or as in 2 Thessalonians 1:9, away from the presence of the Lord. Since God is omnipresent, how can the unsaved sinner be separated from, or away from, the presence of the Lord?

Various past discussions I have had with other believers concerning the presence, or absence, of God toward the unsaved in the lake of fire have led me to make a distinction between God's omnipresence and what I call his effective presence. One might define God's effective presence as "God at work in a person's life."

For example, the Spirit's effective presence in the New Testament church at congregational worship is of one kind, his effective presence in the life of the unsaved (sitting in the same congregation) that he is drawing to Christ is of another kind. The Spirit's effective presence toward the unsaved he is not drawing to Christ is of yet another kind. Those unsaved the Spirit is not drawing to Christ are separated from God. Not separated from God's omnipresence, but separated from his effective presence.

In relation to discussions of the lake of fire, in common terms the unsaved sinner in the lake of fire is separated from God. What is the manner of that separation if (as is the case) God is omnipresent? The answer is God's effective presence is not in the lake of fire.

The lake of fire was designed to inflict suffering as the expression of God's holiness and justice in unceasing wrath toward the unsaved human and fallen angel. The fire was designed to be unquenchable. The lake of fire does what it was designed to do, without God's effective presence. Put another way, in the lake of fire God does not act in grace, mercy, compassion, kindness, or love toward the unsaved in the lake of fire; only in justice and wrath, which by God's design is unquenchable, everlasting, endless. Indeed, if one rejects the grace, mercy, compassion, kindness, and love of God in Jesus Christ, what is left but God's just wrath?

This "effective presence" concept is nothing new. The old theologians always distinguished between God omnipresent, God working, and the manner in which God is working. I have restated their theology as "effective presence."

For me, it is helpful to distinguish between God's effective presence and his omnipresence, especially in certain discussions. In this particular discussion about annihilationism, the words in 2 Thessalonians 1:9, "away from the presence of the Lord," do not describe annihilationism, but the endless (*aiōnios*) ruin (*ólethros*) of the unsaved person endlessly separated from God's effective presence by being cast into the lake of unquenchable fire.

Hebrews 6:2. The Conditionalist says, "Few traditionalists, if any, argue that this verse teaches that God is continually judging for eternity" so what the verse means is "what is eternal is the outcome; God judges, and the judgment is the result."
[https://rethinkinghell.com/2014/01/15/matthew-2546-does-not-prove-eternal-torment-part-1/]

Of course no person interpreting Hebrews 6:2 by the plain and normal meaning of the words in their particular context will argue for "continually judging," in the sense (an Conditionalist caricature) that "God is continually judging for eternity, banging his gavel and repeatedly declaring saved or unsaved the same finite number of existent people." [https://rethinkinghell.com/2014/01/15/matthew-2546-does-not-prove-eternal-torment-part-1/]. The Conditionalist does himself a disservice by resorting to caricature.

What is the context? The Hebrews Writer is speaking to a group of people who have failed to advance beyond the basics of Christian doctrine. He lists those basics. The fact of a judgment with eternal consequences is foundational to the Gospel message [Quiggle, *Hebrews*, 137]. The interpretation the Conditionalist tries to create out of this verse is well-beyond the Hebrews Writer's intent to list, not explain, the basics. The Conditionalist's tactic is to redefine biblical words to support their predetermined doctrine.

The last of the seven scriptures is Jude 7, "as Sodom and Gomorrah, and the cities around them in the same manner with them, having practiced fornication and having followed after strange flesh, are set forth as an example to suffer the penalty of eternal [aiõnios] fire."

There is no mystery here. The punishment of the inhabitants of "Sodom and Gomorrah, and the cities around them" is the "penalty of eternal [aiõnios] fire." The example of unbelief in Israel, Jude 5, and the example of apostasy in the fallen angels, Jude 6, and the example of defilement in Jude 7, reveal God punishes sinners with an everlasting punishment.

The "punishment" of non-existence proposed by the Evangelical Conditionalist is not punishment, it is relief from punishment. That is exactly how the Conditionalist explains his doctrine: a brief duration of punishment in the lake of fire, then non-existence. It is an axiom of rationality and logic that a person who does not exist cannot be punished. Duration is not itself punishment, merely a condition of the punishment.

The punishment in the lake of fire is endless separation from the effective presence of God and the endless experience of God's wrath. Because God himself is the origin and source of all that is holy, loving, kind, compassionate, and merciful, to be separated from God is to be excluded from those things and be subject to God's just wrath. The duration of that separation is *aiōnios*, endless, in the lake of fire.

kólasis (Strong's 2851; G-K 3136).

We have examined one of the three key words in Matthew 25:46, *aiōnios*. Here we will examine *kólasis*, the word translated "punishment." The meaning of *kólasis* is "to punish." The word has judicial punishment in view, not vindictive punishment [Zodhiates, s. v. 2851]. *Kólasis* occurs twice in the New Testament. In Matthew 25:46 the word is used in the sense of judicial vengeance, in the same way English uses the word "penal." Sin is a crime committed by the sinner against a holy God; the sinner is *kólasis*, judicially punished by the holy God for the crime of sin. In 1 John 4:18 the word is used in the sense of judicial punishment with a view to correction: remedial punishment.

> Matthew 25:46, And these will go away into eternal punishment [*kólasis*], but the righteous into eternal life.
>
> 1 John 4:18, There is no terror in love. On the contrary, love completed casts out terror. Because the terror has torment [*kólasis*], the person who has terror does not have completed love.

First John 4:18 is beyond the scope of this chapter [see Quiggle, *John's Epistles*]. In Matthew 25:46, God enacts punishment on the offender. God acts toward sin in one of three ways:

> Retribution, in judicial vengeance for the crime, with no view toward redemption or restoration.
>
> Redemptive, to save the sinner from his sin.
>
> Remedial, to discipline and correct his saved children in order to restore them to righteousness and fellowship.

What is in view in Matthew 25:46 is divine retribution for those human beings and fallen angles who are in continuous rebellion against God. Summing up, Matthew 25:46 looks to endless judicial punishment of the unsaved as divine retribution, in judicial (penal) vengeance for the crime of sin, with no view toward redemption or restoration.

Zōé (Strong's 2222; G-K2437)

The final key word in Matthew 25:46 is *zōé*, life. The word *zōé* occurs 134 times in the New Testament. Word use is divided unevenly between mortal physical life, endless physical life, and that quality of life known as eternal life.

Contrary to the Physicalist-Conditionalist, the source of physical and mental life is not biological, but is from the immaterial essence "life" in the soul. Genesis 2:7 teaches God first formed Adam's physical body from various elements of the earth. God then separately formed the person Adam, his soul, *ex nihilo*, from nothing. God then placed Adam into the physical body and Adam became a living person.

(For a detailed discussion of the animating principle "life" and God's creation of humankind in Adam, see the first chapter heading, "The Humanity of the God-man," subheading, "Life.")

The human soul contains three immaterial substances. These are the animating principle "life"; the essence that defines the person as a human being; the human nature composed of human attributes, which when combined with life experiences form the personality. Just as Adam's physical life began when the person Adam (the soul), entered the inert body. Even so, for all of Adam's descendants (all human beings), physical life ends when the person (the soul) leaves the body.

Scripture never states the dissolution of a human or angel person—the soul is the person. The complete absence in Scripture of the annihilation of the soul is the complete absence of support for the doctrines of annihilationism. The biblical view is once the person comes into existence, that personal existence continues endlessly. "I am," said God at Exodus 3:15, "the God of Abraham, the God of Isaac, and the God of Jacob"; "He is not," said Jesus, "God of the dead but of the living," Mark 12:27, quoting Exodus 3:15. Physical death means the body becomes non-living, but the person continues in active conscious living as a disembodied soul until the resurrection.

Death in Scripture is separation, it is not non-existence. At physical death the soul separates from the body: the body become inert, non-living, decomposing, but the person continues in conscious existence in hades or in heaven. The soul is never non-existent, it is immortal, which is the consequence of possessing the animating principle "life," and of being an immaterial spirit essence. It is worth repeating Scripture never states, examples, or implies the dissolution of the soul, or a means of dissolution for the soul. (For a discussion of Matthew 10:28, see the first chapter heading "The Humanity of the God-man," subheading, "An Immortal Soul.") Just the opposite, Exodus 3:15; Mark 12:27.

In spiritual death—which is the spiritual state of all unsaved persons, whether physically alive, physically dead, or physically resurrected—the unsaved person is separated from God's effective presence: no communion with God, no spiritual perception (1 Corinthians 2:14), no spiritual life.

In this world physical life is mortal: everyone dies physically. What, then, is endless physical life. In a word, it is "immortality." Endless physical immortal life is the destiny of every human being, saved or unsaved. Endless physical life is the consequence of the resurrection of the body. Resurrection may be scripturally defined.

> The reuniting of an individual soul with its original body after physical death has occurred. Resurrection encompasses two processes: 1) God reforms the physically dead body from existing materials and, 2) God causes the disembodied soul originally propagated with that body to join with it and animate it. The soul and resurrected body will continue in that reunited state endlessly.

When the body of the saved person is resurrected, it is re-formed free from the presence of sin, and transformed and glorified to be endlessly incorruptible and physically immortal, 1

Corinthians 15:53. The saved live endlessly in the state of reunited, transformed and glorified, immortal body and soul without sin or corruption.

When the body of the unsaved person is resurrected, it is re-formed to be endlessly corruptible and physically immortal, Revelation 20:14–15; 21:8. In the unsaved, resurrection reunites an immortal sinful soul with a corrupt immortal body to endure endless suffering.

In interpreting Scripture, the Bible student must distinguish between things that differ. Some words, such as the words "eternal life," are used with different meanings in different contexts. When Jesus said, "I give them life eternal; and never no never will they perish for the age," John 10:28, he was not speaking of immortal physical life (cf. John 3:16). We know this because he says of those to whom he gives eternal life "never no never will they perish for the age." Yet, everyone perishes— everyone experiences physical death (except 1 Corinthians 15:51–52; 1 Thessalonians 4:17). So in the John 10:28 context, "life eternal" must not mean immortal physical life. In that context, and others, eternal life is spiritual life: a quality of life God imparts or adds to the believer at salvation, wherein he shares his communicable attributes in a measure suitable to a finite being, enlivening the faculty of spiritual perception, regenerating the soul to born-again. John 5:24 is another verse where spiritual life is in view.

In other contexts, eternal life means immortal physical life. The rich young ruler at Matthew 19:16 was seeking assurance he had immortal physical life in the presence of God after resurrection (cf. Daniel 12:2). Matthew 19:29 looks to immortal physical life. First Timothy 6:19 looks to immortal physical life, "laying up in store for themselves a good foundation for the future, so that they may take hold of that which is genuinely life." The believers to whom Paul was writing already had the quality eternal life, so Paul must be speaking of the quality of one's immortal physical life in the presence of God. "Laying up in store" is a reference to the rewards, 1 Corinthians 3:12–15.

Matthew 25:46, "the righteous [go] into eternal life." Jesus has completed the story of judgment at 25:45: the righteous inherit the kingdom; the unrighteous go into endless punishment. The righteous who inherit the kingdom were saved before the judgment—that is why they inherit the kingdom. They enter the kingdom mortal and born-again. They have the quality of eternal life as a present possession. What then is this "eternal life" in Matthew 25:46?

Eschatological Considerations

Here we divide over eschatology. Reformed eschatology will say these righteous of Matthew 25:46 are entering into the eternal kingdom (Revelation 21–22) after the Great White Throne Judgment (25:31–45), because Reformed eschatology believes in one single judgment, the Great White Throne of Revelation 20:11–15. In Reformed eschatology, the saved and unsaved are judged at the same time. In Reformed eschatology, what is in view at Matthew 25:46 is both the quality of life and the endless duration of life for both saved and unsaved.

The Dispensationalist understands Matthew 25:31–45 as a judgment taking place at the end of the Tribulation period, as part of the inauguration of the Davidic-Messianic-Millennial Kingdom of 2 Samuel 7:13, 16; Psalm 2; Hebrews 10:13 (cf. Psalm 110:1). The judged are all those persons who survived the Tribulation. The outcome of the judgment is who will enter into the millennial kingdom. (Reformed eschatology rejects a Tribulation and rejects an earthly kingdom of the Messiah Jesus Christ, the Davidic-Messianic-Millennial Kingdom, immediately following the Tribulation. In Reformed eschatology this current universe ends like this: Christ returns, final judgment happens, the eternal kingdom begins.)

Only the living saved, Matthew 25:34–40, enter into the kingdom (the resurrected saved are present with the ruler, Jesus Christ). Those living saved entering the Kingdom are born-again, and will continue to be mortal (but have longer lives, Isaiah 65:20), and will have children, just as believers today have children—children who need salvation (hence, Revelation 20:7–10). The story of judgment and inheriting the kingdom is completed at Matthew 25:45. Then, at 25:46, Jesus speaks to the final destination of the sheep: their endless physical and spiritual life in the eternal kingdom after the millennial kingdom.

The Dispensationalist understands Matthew 25:41, 46 as looking toward the final disposition of the goats, who represent the unsaved surviving the Tribulation. The immediate effect of the judgment is the goats do not enter the kingdom. Their final destination is "the eternal fire prepared for the devil and his angels." This does not mean they do not first enter Hades, as do all the unsaved dead prior to the Great White Throne judgment. (Think of Hades as the county jail where the condemned and sentenced prisoner awaits final disposition in the eternal prison of the lake of fire.) There will be a thousand years (the Davidic-Messianic-Millennial Kingdom) between the physical death of the goats (they do not enter the Kingdom) and the final judgment by Christ, Revelation 20:11–13, and then they will go into the endless suffering of the everlasting fire, Revelation 20:14–15, initially prepared for the devil and his angels, but after Adam's sin the final destination of all the unsaved.

Summary

The question this chapter set out to answer was, "Does Matthew 25:46 teach the endless conscious suffering of the unsaved?" The answer is, "Yes, it does."

The Conditionalist teaches eternal punishment is not the duration of the punishment but the duration of the consequences of punishment. Conditionalism proposes the unsaved suffer an indefinite period of torment in the lake of fire and then their existence is ended. That state of non-existence, as though they never existed, is in the Conditionalist's theology "eternal" because they endlessly cease to exist and are never re-created by God into existence. They are annihilated.

To oppose the Conditionalist doctrine, I discussed some important concepts, such as the biblical meaning of life, death, immortality, eternal life, second death, unquenchable, the irrational concept that eternal punishment is the duration of the consequence (non-existence) not the duration of the punishment, the illogical comparison (by the Conditionalist) of endless life with non-existence. The logical comparison is the quality of endless life: endlessly in heaven or endlessly in the lake of fire. I also discussed the Conditionalist's dishonest use of

Augustine's *City of God*.

I argued that the continuing existence of the lake of fire in the new heaven and new earth indicates the purpose of the lake of fire continues in the new heaven and earth. As every sinner that ever lived will be cast into the lake of fire, Revelation 20:15, that continuing purpose of the unquenchable fire must be the endless punishment of those sinners.

I exegeted Matthew 25:46 in context. The conclusion was the contrast between those inheriting the kingdom (Matthew 25:34) and those not inheriting the kingdom (25:41) is not between a state of continuing life and continuing non-existence, but between the continuing life of the saved in the kingdom, first the millennial kingdom, then the eternal kingdom, versus the continuing life of the unsaved, first in hades, then in the "eternal fire prepared for the devil and his angels."

I then examined the key words in Matthew 25:46, which are "eternal (*aiōnios*), punishment (*kólasis*), and life (*zōé*)." The conclusion was the consistent use of *aiōnios* in sixty-four occurrences communicates the idea of endlessness in relation to life, glory, and salvation. The seven seeming exceptions were examined and found to not contradict that conclusion. The use of *aiōnios* in Matthew 25:46 conforms to the use of *aiōnios* all other occurrences: the endless conscious suffering of the unsaved.

I examined punishment, *kólasis*. The meaning is judicial vengeance. In its contextual relationship with *aiōnios* in Matthew 25:46, *kólasis* means the endless judicial retribution of God toward the unsaved.

I examined *zōé*. The basic meaning of this word is "life." I discussed (and reference was made to a discussion in the first chapter) that physical life is the consequence of the soul in the body, physical death the consequence of the soul leaving the body. (In other words, in Scripture death is always separation, never annihilation.) I then looked at several scriptures, showing that *zōé* has in view different aspects of life depending on the word or words in the context in which *zōé* is used. Eternal life is a quality of life. When used with *aiōnios* or *aiōn* the meaning of *zōé* is endless spiritual life, or endless physical life.

The contrast, then, in Matthew 25:46, between *aiōnios kólasis* and *zōé* is the not the life itself, but manner of life. The unsaved will experience a manner of life that is *aiōnios kólasis*, God's endless judicial vengeance against sinners, endlessly separated from the effective presence of God.

The saved will experience a manner of life that is *aiōnios zōé:* endless life as a quality of spiritual life and as incorruptible immortality of body and soul, in the effective presence of God.

Final Word

One of the more helpful books on the endless conscious suffering of the unsaved is W. G. T. Shedd, *The Doctrine of Endless Punishment*. After presenting the "History of the Doctrine," and the "Biblical Argument," Shedd presents the "Rational Argument" [Shedd, *Endless*, 118–169]. Among other rational arguments, he explains: the purpose of the punishment is not remedial or redemptive but judicial retribution; the continuous guilt of the unsaved because unforgiven; there is no repentance in the lake of fire, therefore the sinner continues to sin, therefore the punishment continues.

One might object that there is no sin in the eternal kingdom, and therefore the unsaved in the lake of fire do not continue sinning. There is no sin among the living in the eternal kingdom, but those in the lake of fire are sinners, Revelation 21:8. The essence of the attribute sin in human nature is unceasing rebellion against God, expressed in acts of sinning in mind, soul, and body. Sinning is natural to the sinner. Therefore, as there is no redemption, no regeneration (born-again), no grace, no mercy in the lake of fire, only God's unending wrath, the sinner in the lake of fire continues to do what he or she has always naturally done throughout life, while in hades, and now in the lake of fire: continue to commit acts of sinning in rebellion against God.

To Shedd's list I would add another. The scripture describes the endless conscious life of the saved in the presence of God with the same word used to describe the endless conscious suffering of the unsaved in the lake of fire. That word is *aiōnios*: eternal, endless, forever, eternity.

If there is an end point to the *aiōnios* suffering of the unsaved in the lake of fire, then there is an end point to the *aiōnios* blissful life of the saved in the effective presence of God. The unsaved will endure endless conscious suffering for as long as the saved experience endless conscious eternal life. That endless conscious eternal life of the saved extends into the eternal kingdom, the new heaven and earth, described in Revelation 21–22. So also the endless conscious suffering of the unsaved in the unquenchable, everlasting lake of fire, Revelation 21:8.

Conclusion

The doctrines of Physicalism and Annihilationism existed long before the doctrine of conditional immortality. Physicalism was a Greek philosophy, first attributed to the Greek philosopher Thales (624–545 BC). The word "physicalism" came into modern philosophy in the 1930s. Annihilationism of the human soul was a philosophy recognized by the Greek philosopher Plato (428–347 BC), who explained it, but did not agree with it.

The biblical problem with Annihilationism when introduced into Christianity was what to do with a naturally, intrinsically immortal soul. Conditionalism supplied a reasonable solution. If the soul is as subject to death as the body, then both may be annihilated.

The doctrine of the conditional immortality of the human soul seems to have existed since ca. AD 600. The doctrine has always been associated with annihilationism, and many early writers referred to Conditionalism as Annihilationism. I was able to trace modern Conditionalism to ca. 1928, a development of the late 19th century, but the doctrine began its latest resurgence ca. 1965. Evangelical Conditionalism, at least as a label, is much more recent. Conditionalism has always been associated with some form of annihilationism.

B.B. Warfield wrote on conditional immortality, and annihilationism proper, in the 1908 edition of the *New Schaff-Herzog Encyclopedia of Religious Knowledge*. He cites works on Conditionalism published in 1853, 1854, 1857, and later in the 19th century. Warfield cites Salmond (1838–1905) on the first appearance of annihilationism in Christianity.

> The earliest appearance of a genuinely annihilationist theory in extant Christian literature is to be found apparently in the African apologist Arnobius, at the opening of the fourth century. [Salmond, "The Christian Doctrine of Immortality," Edinburgh, 1901, pp. 473—474."
>
> [https://thirdmill.org/magazine/article.asp/link/bb_warfield%5Ebb_warfield.Annihilationism.html/at/Annihilationism]

I have (a reprint of) Salmond's book in my personal library. Salmond says Arnobius (AD 255–330) was "the first writer of note certainly known to us to have been of that way of thinking." Salmon's chapter 2, in his final section, "Conclusions," title, "Doctrines of Annihilationism and Conditional Immortality" is certainly worth reading. [Salmond, 473–499.]

To call the physicalism+annihilationism+conditionalism that is today's Conditionalism, "Evangelical," is grossly lacking in honesty. Evangelical is defined as "according to the teaching of the gospel or the Christian religion." Evangelical Conditionalism is neither.

The Christian gospel message is that salvation in this mortal life from the eternal penalty due sins after this mortal life, is by having faith during this mortal life in God and God's testimony of the way of salvation. Evangelical Conditionalism's plan of salvation is this: after resurrection, some are given by God the gift of immortality and others are not. From chapter 1.

> Conditionalism is the view that life is the Creator's

provisional gift to all, which will ultimately be granted forever to the saved and revoked forever from the unsaved. When the gift of life is ultimately granted forever, we call that immortality. We also call it eternal life. Salvation, on our view, is salvation to everlasting life with God. Simultaneously, it is salvation from a permanent death (termination of life forever; final loss of being).
[https://rethinkinghell.com/2019/07/20/conditional-immortality-meaning-best-label/]

The basis for the reward of immortality is defined by Evangelical Conditionalism as God elected some to receive immortality *after* resurrection. That is not biblical salvation. That is not the gospel. That is not evangelical. The label "Evangelical Conditionalism" is an oxymoron insulting the intelligence of every believer in Jesus Christ as Savior.

Evangelical Conditionalism is not the historic orthodox Christian religion of Christ and the apostles. Its gospel is wrong. The Physicalist and Substance Dualist sects of Evangelical Conditionalism deny the biblical understanding of the incarnation.

In Physicalist-Conditionalism, God stopped being God and became human in the incarnation. In Physicalist-Conditionalism, when the Christ died on the cross, the incarnate person ceased to exist because life is only material, the person an effect of living biology.

In Substance Dualist-Conditionalism, when the Christ died on the cross, the incarnate person ceased to exist because the human soul of the Christ went to sleep. That is, because the consciousness of Jesus Christ is a blending deity and humanity, when the humanity slept the Christ ceased to function as an incarnate being.

In all sects of Conditionalism the human soul is as mortal as the human body during this mortal life. In Physicalist-Conditionalism the mortal soul ceases to exist at physical death. In Substance-Dualist-Physicalism the soul is relieved of the burden of conscious existence by a "sleep" that endures from physical death to resurrection.

The heresy is named "Conditionalism" because in their doctrine immortality of soul and body is "conditional" during this mortal life. "Conditional" means no one has it. Only after physical death and resurrection will some be given immortality, while others will be punished and annihilated, made non-existent. What the Jehovah Witnesses call "terminal punishment." What the Mormons call "outer darkness."

The concept of conditional immortality and annihilation permeates many heresies, including the heresy known as Evangelical Conditionalism. Christianity has always vigorously rejected Physicalism, Annihilationism, and Conditionalism in those random times and places where it has popped up to deceive others. As then, so also now, historic orthodox Christianity rejects the heresy of Physicalism, Annihilationism, and Evangelical Conditionalism

The Evangelical Conditionalists do have a doctrinal statement. [https://rethinkinghell.com/statement/]

> 1. Conditionalism is the view that life is the Creator's provisional gift to all, which will ultimately be granted

forever to the saved and revoked forever from the unsaved.

2. Evangelical Conditionalists believe that the saved in Christ will receive glory, honor and immortality, being raised with an incorruptible body to inherit eternal life (Romans 2:7).

3. The unsaved will be raised in shame and dishonor, to face God and receive the just condemnation for their sins. When the penalty is carried out, they will be permanently excluded from eternal life by means of a final death, implicating the whole person in a destruction of human life and being (Matthew 10:28).

4. The Holy Scriptures as originally given by God, divinely inspired, infallible, entirely trustworthy; and the supreme authority in all matters of faith and conduct...One God, eternally existent in three persons, Father, Son, and Holy Spirit...

5. Our Lord Jesus Christ, God manifest in the flesh, His virgin birth, His sinless human life, His divine miracles, His vicarious and atoning death, His bodily resurrection, His ascension, His mediatorial work, and His Personal return in power and glory...

6. The Salvation of lost and sinful man through the shed blood of the Lord Jesus Christ by faith apart from works, and regeneration by the Holy Spirit...

7 The Holy Spirit, by whose indwelling the believer is enabled to live a holy life, to witness and work for the Lord

Jesus Christ...

8. The Unity of the Spirit of all true believers, the Church, the Body of Christ...

9. The Resurrection of both the saved and the lost; they that are saved unto the resurrection of life, they that are lost unto the resurrection of damnation.

Some in their doctrine conforms to historic orthodox Christianity; but they do not believe in it. Number four might as well use the Mormon's statement, "only insofar as properly interpreted," because the interpretations Evangelical Conditionalism applies to the "Holy Scriptures as originally given by God" is far and away from historic orthodox Christianity.

Numbers 6 and 7 are blatantly deceptive. How can there be regeneration without salvation, which in Evangelical Conditionalism does not occur until *after* resurrection. How can the Holy Spirit indwell the believer, when there are no believers in Evangelical Conditionalism in the biblical sense, and the Holy Spirit only indwells after salvation, which in Evangelical Conditionalism does not occur until *after* resurrection.

Evangelical Conditionalism claims their statement of faith is just like others that are "characteristically evangelical, such as that of the World Evangelical Alliance." I looked at the World Evangelical Alliance statement of faith. Numbers 1–3 of Evangelical Conditionalism are not there. But of course, on the Evangelical Conditionalism website, numbers 1–3 are deceptively placed apart from their "evangelical" doctrines. But that numbers 1–3 are part of Evangelical Conditionalism's doctrine is apparent with even a casual inspection. Deception is a characteristic of heresy.

Another deception. Evangelical Conditionalism exactly quotes the World Evangelical Alliance item 7,

> The Resurrection of both the saved and the lost; they that are saved unto the resurrection of life, they that are lost unto the resurrection of damnation.

But what Evangelical Conditionalism fails to say is its understanding of "lost unto the resurrection of damnation" is not the same as the World Evangelical Alliance. The words are the same, but Evangelical Conditionalism has redefined "damnation" to mean the non-existence of annihilation.

Evangelical Conditionalism-Physicalism-Annihilationism—that is its true name—is neither evangelical nor Christian. I urge any caught up in that heresy to carefully consider the arguments in this book.

Sources

Ames, William. *The Marrow of Theology.* 1629, Reprinted Durham, NC: The Labyrinth Press, 1698.

Dickson, David. *Truth's Victory Over Error, or the True Principles of the Christian Religion*. n.d. Reprinted, Edmonton, AB, Canada: Still Water Revival Books. n.d.

Dyson, Freeman. "How We Know," The New York Review of Books 10 March 2011.

Goodspeed, Edgar J. Translator. *The Apocrypha*. 1938, Reprinted, New York: Vintage Books, 1989.

Hamilton, Victor P. *The Book of Genesis, Chapters 1–17*, NICNT. Grand Rapids, MI: Eerdmans, 1990.

Harris, R. Laird; Gleason L. Archer, Jr.; and Bruce K. Waltke. *Theological Wordbook of the Old Testament*. 2 vols. Chicago, IL: Moody Press, 1980.

Harrison, Everett, F., ed. *Baker's Dictionary of Theology*. Grand Rapids, MI: Baker Book House, 1960.

Hodge, Charles. *Systematic Theology*. 1871–1873. Reprinted, Grand Rapids, MI: Eerdmans Publishing, 1981.

Kittel, Gerhard, and Gerhard Friedrich. *Theological Dictionary of the New Testament*. 10 vols. Translated by Geoffrey W. Bromiley. Grand Rapids, MI: Eerdmans Publishing, 1967.

Lim, Joungbin. Article, *A Physicalist View Of The Passion Of The Christ.*

Moulton, J. H., and G. Milligan. *Vocabulary of the Greek Testament*. 1930. Reprinted, Peabody, MA: Hendrickson Publishers, 1997.

O'Brien, Peter T. *The Epistle to the Philippians, A Commentary on* the Greek Text. New International Greek Text Commentary. Grand Rapids, MI: William B. Eerdmans Publishing, 1991.

Quiggle, James D. *A Private Commentary on the Bible: John's Epistles*. Amazon/KDP, 2016.

_____. *A Private commentary on the Bible: Mark's Gospel*. Amazon/KDP, 2019.

_____. *A Private Commentary on the Bible: Matthew's Gospel*. Amazon/KDP, 2017.

_____. *A Private Commentary on the Bible: Philippians*. Amazon/KDP, 2020.

_____. *Adam and Eve, A Biography and Theology.*

_____. *Biblical Essays IV*. Amazon/KDP, 2021.

_____. *Dictionary of Doctrinal Words*. Amazon/KDP, 2020.

_____. *Did Jesus Go To Hell?*

_____. *Dispensational Eschatology, An Explanation and Defense of the Doctrine*. Amazon/KDP, 2013.

_____. *Four Voices, One Testimony*. Amazon/KDP, 2022.

_____. *God Became Incarnate*. Amazon/KDP, 2014.

_____. *Life, Death, Eternity*. Amazon/KDP, 2019.

_____. *Thirty-six Essentials of the Christian Faith*. Amazon/KDP, 2021.

Robertson, A. T. *Word Pictures in the New Testament*. Vol. 6. Nashville, TN: Broadman Press, 1932.

Charles C. Ryrie. *Basic Theology*. 1986. Reprinted, Chicago, IL: Moody Publishers, 1999.

_____. *Dispensationalism*. Chicago, IL: Moody Press, 1995.

Salmond, S.D.F. *The Christian Doctrine of Immortality*. 1895. Reprinted, Miami FL: HardPress Publishing, n.d.

Schaff, Philip. *The Creeds of Christendom*. 1931. Reprinted,

Grand Rapids, MI: Baker Book House, 1983.

_____. *Nicene and Post–Nicene Fathers, First Series*. Vol. 2. *City of God, Christian Doctrine*. 1887. Reprinted, Peabody, MA: Hendrickson Publishers, 1999.

Shedd, W. G. T. *Dogmatic Theology*. 1863. 3 vols. Reprinted, Nashville, TN: Thomas Nelson Publishers, 1980.

_____. *The Doctrine of Endless Punishment*. 1885. Reprinted, Carlisle, PA: Banner of Truth Trust, 1986.

Silva, Moisés. Revision Editor. *New International Dictionary of New Testament Theology and Exegesis*. Grand Rapids, MI: Zondervan, 2014.

_____. *Philippians*. 2nd ed. Baker Exegetical Commentary on the New Testament. Grand Rapids, MI: Baker Academic, 2005.

Warfield, Benjamin B. *The Savior of the World.* 1916. Reprinted, Carlisle, PA: Banner of Truth Trust, 1991.

Zodhiates, Spiros. *The Complete Word Study Dictionary: New Testament*. Revised. Chattanooga, TN: AMG Publishers, 1993.

www.ingramcontent.com/pod-product-compliance
Lightning Source LLC
Chambersburg PA
CBHW060830050426
42453CB00008B/642